The Feminine Genius of Catholic Theology

The Feminine Genius of Catholic Theology

Matthew Levering

t &t clark

Published by T&T Clark International
A Continuum Imprint

The Tower Building   80 Maiden Lane
11 York Road   Suite 704
London   New York
SE1 7NX   NY 10038

www.continuumbooks.com

British Library Cataloguing-in-Publication Data

A catalogue record for this book is available from the British Library

ISBN: 978-0-5676-3306-4 (hardback)
978-0-5671-9686-6 (paperback)

Typeset by Deanta Global Publishing Services, Chennai, India
Printed and bound in India

To Susan Keefe

CONTENTS

ACKNOWLEDGMENTS

I should first thank Tom Kraft of T. & T. Clark for his patient encouragement of this book. He and the readers he assembled— Susan Frank Parsons and an anonymous reader—offered insights and guidance that made possible its publication. A special thanks to Susan Parsons for her generosity with her time. Jason Pannone, who directs the library of Harvard's department of philosophy, took time from his busy schedule to read and critique the entire manuscript, for which I am very grateful. Among those who have inspired my interest in the women mystical theologians, I should mention Louis Roy, OP, Ralph Martin, and my beloved mother Patty Levering. Over the years I have taught the writings of various "women mystics," and this past year I had the opportunity to devote an entire course to their works. My students in this course were senior undergraduates, and I benefited greatly from their enthusiasm and insight. Kyle Rodden deserves a special mention. Thanks to Jason Heron, a highly talented doctoral student, for compiling the index. This book would never have been written without my amazing wife Joy Levering. I praise God for the blessings of being married to Joy.

During my Master's studies at Duke Divinity School, Professor Susan Keefe, a person of deep prayer, introduced me to the writings of the women mystical theologians. I gained a real understanding of how Edith Stein could have picked up Teresa of Avila's autobiography by chance, read it through at a sitting, and shortly thereafter been baptized as a Catholic. The present book is therefore dedicated to Susan Keefe in gratitude and appreciation. Against the trends of the academy, she taught me that "we look not to the things that are seen but to the things that are unseen; for the things that are seen are transient, but the things that are unseen are eternal" (2 Cor 4:18).

Introduction

Let me begin by recalling the novel that, when I was in high school, introduced me to theology and theologians. This novel was *Middlemarch* by Mary Ann Evans, whose pen name was George Eliot. In *Middlemarch*, the heroine, Dorothea Brooke, is a beautiful young woman who at first idealizes the life and work of a middle-aged theologian of her acquaintance, the Reverend Isaac Casaubon. A devout Christian, Dorothea wants to do heroic deeds for Christ, dreams of becoming a martyr, and renounces simple pleasures so as to focus on higher things. She has memorized much of Blaise Pascal's *Pensées* as well as the writings of the Anglican theologian Jeremy Taylor, and she enjoyed a small book by Casaubon on the topic of biblical cosmology. Casaubon is presently at work on what he hopes will be his *magnum opus*, a key to the entirety of the world's mythological systems that will reveal their original essence. Dorothea marries Causabon, but she is quickly disillusioned. By the end of the book, after Causabon dies, she chooses between an idealistic young artist and a bold physician-scientist, both atheists. She marries the latter and discovers in herself a deep inner strength, quite different from her youthful yearning for God.

In certain ways, the story parallels Mary Ann Evans's own loss of religious faith as a young woman and her discovery of herself as an author in her own right. Intriguingly, however, the novel begins with a "Prelude" that extols the bravery and passion of St. Teresa of Avila. Had the Prelude taken the writings of the women mystical theologians more seriously, *Middlemarch* would have been a powerful novel in quite a different way. The portrait of Casaubon, for example, exemplifies the academic theologians whom Catherine of Siena criticized for "chasing after a multiplicity of books, never tasting the marrow of Scripture because they have let go of the light by which Scripture was formed and proclaimed."[1]

---

[1] Catherine of Siena, *The Dialogue*, trans. Suzanne Noffke, O.P. (Mahwah, NJ: Paulist Press, 1980), p. 157.

In this light, the present book introduces Catholic theology through the writings of the great women mystical theologians. Although in this Introduction I will offer some very brief background about their lives, this book is not a historical analysis of their writings, but rather is a constructive synthesis organized around the central themes of Catholic theology. The book does not attempt to set forth the biblical and historical foundations of Catholic theology. Rather, doctrines are the core of this book, and the goal of the book is to inspire living contact with the realities that these doctrines convey.

Most women mystical theologians were not theologically trained in the modern sense of the term. They often received revelations from the Lord, and they described their own spiritual experiences. Susan Frank Parsons points out that the theological life—the Christian life—involves "submission to suffering and self-sacrifice," and so in these theologians' lives we should expect to see "the ways in which their lives came to embody Christ's own life, and in some cases their immense personal anguish at what they were made to bear for Christ—all for the sake of disclosing in the fullness of their own person the truths of faith that were being revealed to them, put upon them, handed over to them."[2] As we would expect, the Church has acclaimed many of these theologians as saints. Since the starting point of Catholic theology is not pure rationality but faith in Jesus Christ, crucified and risen from the dead, saints are the true theologians. Their lives reveal that they have grasped the mystery of salvation. If anyone can introduce Catholic theology, surely they can. With the saints, we must become "feminine" or receptive in relation to God rather than imagining ourselves to be self-sufficient.

Reality evokes our wonder. How is it that intelligent beings are roaming around a planet in the midst of a universe marked by such delicate beauty? Is it not wondrous that a finite being such as the universe exists and coheres? Theology recognizes the Creator God as the loving source of the wondrous outpouring of finite beings that constitutes the universe. To discover that the Creator is himself interpersonal love—Father, Son, and Holy Spirit, one God—and that this Creator restores his wounded rational creatures by coming among them in supreme love, so that they may share in his eternal embrace of infinite wisdom and love, is a discovery that calls forth joy.

---

[2]Author's email conversation with Susan Frank Parsons, July 15, 2011.

Could reality be so wondrous that we are eternally loved, that everything comes from love and leads to love rather than coming from nothingness and leading to annihilation? The Catholic theologians upon whose writings I depend in this book knew that it is so. Chapter 1 explores the mystery of the triune God, who is an infinite communion of love, and who creates us out of sheer love. Even now, the Father, Son, and Holy Spirit dwell within believers. Chapter 2 addresses Jesus Christ, who comes to fulfill God's covenants with Israel and bring about the forgiveness of sins and the reconciliation of the whole world to God. As the incarnate Son of God, Jesus is able to restore the love relationship that humans had wounded by sin. Chapter 3 explores creation and providence. All created things bear traces of their Trinitarian Creator, and humans and angels are made in the image of God. God cares for everything he has made, so that his providence guides us to union with him. Although God permits sin, God's wise plan for the good of his creatures cannot be frustrated. Chapter 4 examines sin, whose terrible depths must be confronted clearly. Humans would not need a Redeemer if we had not got ourselves into a situation of terrible alienation from God and from each other. Faced with violence and death, we desperately need God to recreate us in love. Chapter 5 treats the sacraments, which give us a participation in Jesus' Cross and thereby heal our sins and configure us to Jesus' supreme love. The sacraments are fundamentally God's work in us, rather than our work; but God enables us to participate in these acts of worship so as to share in his redemptive work.

Chapter 6 turns to the Church, which is built up by Christ and the Holy Spirit through the sacraments. In the Church, the body of Christ, we see not only God's amazing generosity in drawing us into his life of love, but also God's humility in giving himself into weak and sinful human hands. To counter our pride, we must learn to receive Jesus' gifts in community rather than grasping them on our own terms as individuals. Chapter 7 examines the virtues that pertain to Christian life, beginning with faith. In order to love God and neighbor even in difficult circumstances, we need not merely charity, but also justice, fortitude, obedience, patience, humility, detachment, temperance, and so forth. These virtues enable us to obey God's wise law of love.

Chapter 8 examines the role of the Virgin Mary and the saints. The Virgin Mary is prepared in sanctity to be the Mother of God, a mission that includes following Jesus to the Cross and thus requires great love. She is the mother of all those who are sons and daughters in her Son. Christ wills that in loving him, we also love and pray for each other, and so Mary and the saints love and pray for us. To relate to Christ never means to relate to him exclusively. Chapter 9 attends to the life of prayer that Jesus calls us to undertake. Vocal prayer leads into an interior communion with the Lord, in which our mind is concentrated entirely upon him. Through the gift of contemplation, God takes over our minds so that we get a taste of him that is not merely our own thoughts. In liturgical prayer, especially in the liturgy of the Eucharist, we perceive God's incredible generosity and humility as he inclines himself toward us and unites us to himself through Christ and the Holy Spirit.

Lastly, Chapter 10 depicts the ineffable consummation of the life of prayer and charity, namely eternal life with God the Trinity in the communion of saints. When all has taken place that God has ordained, God will bring the world to an end. Christ will come to raise the dead and to judge all things, putting everything to rights. The eternal life of the blessed will be marked by the peace of dwelling together in God's infinite communion of wisdom and love.

From Egeria through Mother Teresa

Before we begin, let me briefly identify the women whose writings form the basis of these ten chapters. With the exception of one voice from the patristic period, they come from the second millennium of the Church's history. They take part in the liturgical and intellectual task of appropriating biblical revelation in light of the patristic inheritance. In chronological order, they are Egeria (late 300s–early 400s), Hildegard of Bingen (1098–1179), Elisabeth of Schönau (1128–64), Mechthild of Magdeburg (c. 1208–c. 1282/94), Hadewijch (1200s), Angela of Foligno (c. 1248–1309), Gertrud the Great of Helfta (1256–c. 1302), Birgitta of Sweden (1302–73), Julian of Norwich (1342–c. 1423), Catherine of Siena (1347–80), Catherine of Genoa (1447–1510), Teresa of Avila (1515–82), Jane de Chantal (1572–1641), Louise de Marillac (1591–1660), Juana Inés de la Cruz (1648–95), Elizabeth Ann Seton (1774–1821), Elisabeth Leseur (1866–1914), Thérèse of Lisieux (1873–97), Elizabeth of the Trinity (1880–1906), Teresa Benedicta of the Cross/

Edith Stein (1891–1942), Maria Faustina Kowalska (1905–38), and Mother Teresa of Calcutta (1910–97). Of these, the book's central protagonists are Hildegard, Catherine of Siena, Julian, and Thérèse. What we know of Egeria, we glean from her *Diary of a Pilgrimage*. She appears to have lived in the late fourth or early fifth century. She seems to have been a vowed religious, writing to fellow religious sisters; and she is thought to have been from Spain. Since her party of travelers received military protection, she must have been from an eminent family.

Hildegard was the founder and abbess of a Benedictine abbey in Bingen, in modern-day Germany. Her parents, members of the nobility, gave her at the age of eight to serve as a handmaid and companion to another noblewoman who had adopted a solitary life; their hermitage soon expanded to become a Benedictine abbey linked to a nearby monastery, St. Disibod. Hildegard began writing her works at age 43, when as abbess of her community she received a mystical experience that opened Scripture to her. Her *Scivias* were read and enthusiastically promoted by Pope Eugenius III in 1148.

Elisabeth of Schönau knew Hildegard personally; her abbey in Schönau was close to the abbey that Hildegard established at Rupertsberg. Elisabeth's writings sought in particular to refute the Catharists, a dualist movement that was then active in the Rhineland. Her brother Ekbert, a deacon in Bonn who eventually became a priest and monk, was the one who wrote down her mystical visions.

Mechthild of Magdeburg, born into a noble family in the archdiocese of Magdeburg (in modern-day Germany), was not trained in Latin or in theology. She appears to have belonged to a beguine house, that is, a community of women vowed to poverty, chastity, and religious devotion but not in an approved religious order. She received encouragement from Heinrich of Halle, a Dominican priest and her confessor, to write about her mystical experiences. She spent her final years at the Cistercian abbey in Helfta, where she influenced the young Gertrud the Great.

Hadewijch also was a beguine who lived in the thirteenth century. Since her life was not written and since her writings are generally not autobiographical, little is known about her. Her familiarity with Latin, rhetoric, astronomy, and theory of music shows her to have been well educated. She held a position of spiritual authority in her community, but eventually she seems to have been separated from her community, perhaps under the charge of teaching quietism. Her love mysticism is influenced by the twelfth-century Victorines, especially William of Saint Thierry.

Angela of Foligno was born a few miles from Assisi, in the town of Foligno. She was married and had several children. A wealthy woman, she experienced a powerful conversion in her mid-thirties and, after the death of her husband and children, gave away her wealth and property. Shortly thereafter, she made profession in the Third Order of St. Francis and devoted herself to prayer and service. Her spiritual testimonies were written down by Brother Arnaldo, a Franciscan who was related to her.

Gertrud the Great of Helfta was received into the Cistercian abbey at Helfta at the age of four, and she lived all her life there. At the abbey she obtained an excellent education in Latin and the liberal arts, and she was well versed in Scripture and the Fathers of the Church. A conversion experience at the age of 25 focused her attention entirely on God. Her life of prayer flowed from this experience. She herself wrote some of her works, and she dictated other writings over a period of twenty years.

Birgitta of Sweden, a cousin of King Magnus Eriksson, married Ulf of Ulvasa at age thirteen. They had eight children together, and by the time of his death in 1344 they had been married for almost thirty years. Her first spiritual guide was Matthias of Linköping, who translated the Bible into Old Swedish. As the Black Plague approached, Birgitta fled Sweden for Rome, where she lived for the rest of her life. In addition to her prophetic writings and her efforts to bring the papal court from Avignon back to Rome, she is known for founding the Order of the Most Holy Savior (Birgittines).

Julian of Norwich spent most of her life as an anchoress in a cell attached to the parish church of Conisford, in Norwich (England). As an anchoress, she had a maidservant to assist her and she was supported by bequests from the community. Her exact dates of birth and death are unknown, and we know nothing significant about her family, although she was well educated. Her revelations began in her thirties after she was cured of a serious illness. Her understanding of these revelations deepened over time, as can be seen by comparing the "long text" of the revelations with the "short text."

Catherine of Siena, born in Siena, was the twenty-fourth child of a wool dyer and his wife. Her family lived close to the church and cloister of San Domenico, and Catherine became a Dominican at the age of 18. Three years later she became a leading member of the "Mantellate," a group of women who, while affiliated with the Dominicans and wearing a religious habit, lived at home rather than in community. Catherine joined actively in their mission of service to the poor and sick. In her late twenties, she intervened in Italian politics and worked to reform the lives of the clergy. She died soon after the election of an antipope, whom she opposed to no avail.

Born into a noble family, Catherine of Genoa married Giulano Adorno at age 15. Her marriage was at first a painfully lonely one, until she experienced a powerful conversion. After her husband underwent bankruptcy, he became a Third Order Franciscan. They focused their work together on caring for the poor and sick. Catherine eventually became director of a large charitable hospital linked to a smaller Franciscan dispensary. During these years, she experienced extraordinary mystical ecstasies, especially during Lent and Advent. Her best known writing concerns purgatory.

Teresa of Avila was born during the reign of Ferdinand and Isabella, and she lived both at the high point of the Spanish Empire and in the midst of the Protestant Reformation and the Spanish Inquisition. Her mother died when Teresa was 13, and Teresa entered a Carmelite monastery at age 20. She became ill, however, and had to recover at home for a number of years. Returning to the Carmelites, she received extraordinary spiritual experiences and wrote numerous works. She was a leader in the order's renewal, and she established many new houses of Carmel throughout Spain.

Born in Dijon, Jane of Chantal married Baron Christophe de Rabutin-Chantal at age twenty, and she had six children, four of whom survived infancy. Their happy marriage came to an end two weeks after the birth of her last child, when her husband died in a hunting accident. A few years later Jane heard Bishop Francis de Sales preach a series of Lenten sermons, and he became her spiritual director and friend. In 1610 she cofounded with him a congregation for women called the Visitation of Holy Mary. For the rest of her life, Jane served as the Mother Superior of the congregation, and she oversaw the establishment of more than eighty houses of the Visitation.

Born into a politically powerful family, Louise de Marillac did not know her mother, who was a paramour of her father Louis de

Marillac. Louise was educated at the abbey of Poissy, near Paris; her aunt was a Dominican nun there. As a young woman Louise sought to join the Daughters of the Passion in Paris, but was denied admission. Instead, she accepted an arranged marriage to Antoine Le Gras, and at age 22 she gave birth to their son. Her husband died when Louise was 34. Around this time Louise met Vincent de Paul, and in 1633 they cofounded the Daughters of Charity, with Louise as Mother Superior.

Juana Inés de la Cruz was also an illegitimate child, born in the village of Nepantla, Mexico and raised by her mother and grandparents. She learned to read as young child and at the age of eight composed a short play for the feast of Corpus Christi. Her mother's sister had married a wealthy merchant, and through this connection Juana was presented at court in Mexico City. She became a lady-in-waiting to the wife of Mexico's viceroy, and was acclaimed for her poetry and playwriting. She entered the Order of St. Jerome in the prestigious convent of St. Paula at age twenty. Her collected works were published in Spain during her lifetime.

Elizabeth Ann Seton was born in New York City and grew up on her uncle's farm in New Rochelle, New York. At age nineteen she married William Seton. They had five children together and their marriage was a happy one, but William died from tuberculosis after less than ten years of marriage. After his death, Elizabeth became attracted to Catholicism, and she converted in 1808. Soon after, she founded a school for girls near Saint Mary's College/Seminary in Baltimore, and at the same time she founded a religious community, the Sisters of Charity of St. Joseph's.

Born into a wealthy family, Elisabeth Leseur married Félix Leseur at the age of 23. Although their marriage remained childless, it was a happy one, despite the fact that Elisabeth was often in ill health and despite their disagreement about faith in Christ. Félix was an atheist who wrote for leading French anticlerical journals. In 1903, while on pilgrimage in Rome, Elisabeth received a spiritual experience that profoundly renewed her commitment to faith. After her death, Félix read her writings, especially her journal, and was inspired to become not only a believer but a Dominican priest.

Thérèse of Lisieux's parents, who were beatified in 2008, sought to enter religious life before meeting each other and marrying in 1858. Thérèse was their ninth and last child; five children survived infancy. Thérèse sought to enter the Carmelites at age 15, but encountered opposition because of her young age. With the support of her father, she went to the bishop of Bayeux and then to Rome to seek approval for her early entrance. When Pope Leo XIII gave his approval, she joined the Carmelites at age 15. She lived there nine years, until her death from tuberculosis.

Elizabeth of the Trinity also was a French Carmelite. Her father, a retired military captain, died when she was seven. At the age of ten she received a powerful spiritual experience during Mass, and at 14 she made a vow of perpetual virginity so as to consecrate her life to Jesus. Having read with great joy Thérèse of Lisieux's autobiography, Elizabeth entered the Dijon Carmel at age 21. She died only five years later.

Raised in a large Jewish family by her widowed mother, Teresa Benedicta of the Cross (Edith Stein) studied philosophy at the University of Breslau for two years, and then moved to the University of Göttingen to study with the founder of phenomenology, Edmund Husserl, whose research assistant she became. After converting to Catholicism in 1932, she taught for eight years at a women's college directed by Dominican sisters, and then taught briefly in Münster before joining the Carmelites in 1935. She lived in the Cologne Carmel until Nazi persecution of the Jews led her to the Carmel of Echt, in Holland, in 1938. The Nazis arrested her in 1942 and sent her to Auschwitz and the gas chamber.

Maria Faustina Kowalska was born into a poor farming family in the village of Głogowiec, Poland, and she left home at fourteen to serve as a domestic servant in the cities of Aleksandrów and Łódź. At the age of 20 she joined the Congregation of Sisters of Our Lady of Mercy, in Warsaw. Almost immediately she received a vision of Christ as the King of Mercy, with rays of mercy coming forth from his heart. He commanded her to paint this image and title it "Jesus, I trust in you;" and he instructed her that the first day after Easter should become the Feast of Mercy. She died of tuberculosis just as World War II was taking shape.

Mother Teresa of Calcutta was born in Skopje, Yugoslavia, of Albanian parents. She was educated at a government school and was active in the Catholic Sodality. At the age of eighteen she volunteered to go on mission to India, and she joined the Loreto Sisters. For almost 20 years, she taught geography at a high school in Calcutta, and she also served as Principal. Inspired by a profound spiritual experience, she asked permission in 1946 to leave the cloister and work in the Calcutta slums, and her request was granted two years later. She then founded the Missionaries of Charity.

...

This book is not about the lives of these women, but about Catholic doctrine as seen largely through their eyes. Their writings show the lived unity of faith and doctrine, in the liturgical, ascetical, and prayerful encounter with the living God. These great women knew doctrines both intellectually and through their own experience of divine realities. Always pointing away from themselves and toward the crucified and risen Lord, they serve as guides into the greatest mysteries of existence. As the Second Vatican Council observes, "Doctrinal training should not have the mere communication of ideas as its objective, but a genuine and profound formation of the students."[3] This formation in Catholic theology takes place within the communion of saints, a communion that the novelist Flannery O'Connor describes as the "action by which charity grows invisibly among us, entwining the living and the dead."[4]

As an introduction to Catholic theology, this book should be read in tandem with Scripture, and alongside other theological and philosophical resources. Although the present book addresses numerous biblical themes, I do not quote Scripture directly here; nor am I able here to detail the theological contributions of the Fathers or show historically how the apostolic deposit of faith was illumined by their successors over the centuries. Nonetheless, I hope that readers will find here something of the "marrow" of Catholic theology.

---

[3] *Optatam Totius*, § 17, in *Vatican Council II*, Vol. 1: *The Conciliar and Post Conciliar Documents*, new revised edition, ed. Austin Flannery, O.P. (Northport, NY: Costello Publishing Company, 1996), p. 721.
[4] Flannery O'Connor, "Introduction to *A Memoir of Mary Ann*," in O'Connor, *Mystery and Manners: Occasional Prose*, selected and edited by Sally and Robert Fitzgerald (New York: Farrar, Straus & Giroux, 1969), pp. 213–28, at 228.

1

God the Trinity

Christians worship one God who is three Persons: Father, Son, and Holy Spirit. Theology is primarily the study of this God. But how do we know anything about "God"? Are there other Gods to worship? What could it possibly mean to worship one God who is three? Even if one could somehow be three, cannot we simply worship the one God and leave it at that?

With these questions in view, let us begin with Catherine of Siena's praise of the Trinity: "You, eternal Trinity, are the craftsman; and I your handiwork have come to know that you are in love with the beauty of what you have made, since you made of me a new creation in the blood of your Son. O abyss! O eternal Godhead! O deep sea! What more could you have given me than the gift of your very self?"[1] To be a creature is to come into existence out of nothing: we do not have to be, and the finite existence that we have is a sheer gift. God explains to Catherine, "I am who I am [Exod 3.14], whereas you have no being at all of yourselves. What being you have is my doing; I am the Creator of everything that has any share in being."[2] Supposing that the universe were an infinite set of finite existing things, even this infinite set would have to receive its existence from another. Finite being cannot cause itself: it can only come from an infinite Creator.

The love of the eternal Godhead for his creatures is expressed by Julian of Norwich. God "created everything for love, and by the

---

[1] Catherine of Siena, *The Dialogue*, trans. Suzanne Noffke, O.P. (Mahwah, NJ: Paulist Press, 1980), p. 365.
[2] Ibid., p. 56.

same love it is preserved, and always will be without end."[3] The mystery of why any creature exists is rooted in God's love. The love that appears in the new creation in Christ Jesus also manifests itself in the creation. The amazing abundance of the universe, the extraordinary complexity and beauty of beings, the fact that we live and move and know, all have their root in God's creative love. After praising Christ's Cross and his Incarnation in the womb of Mary, Julian praises God as "the blessed divinity, that always was and is and shall be, almighty, all wisdom and all love."[4] Since God is infinite love, he is infinite good. Indeed, says Julian, "God is everything which is good, as I see, and the goodness which everything has is God."[5] The goodness of finite beings participates in and points to the infinite goodness of the Creator. God's "goodness is full and complete, and in it is nothing lacking."[6]

With "her mind's eye steadily fixed on the divine majesty," Catherine cries out: "O eternal Father! O fiery abyss of charity! O eternal beauty, O eternal wisdom, O eternal goodness, O eternal mercy! O hope and refuge of sinners! O immeasurable generosity! O eternal, infinite Good! O mad lover!"[7] These praises lead her frequently to contemplate God's providence, his eternal plan for ordering his creatures to union with himself. She says of herself that she has "tasted and seen the abyss of supreme eternal providence."[8] When God creates, he does so with a purpose and a plan that he will bring to fruition, since his eternity means that he is not in time with us: he stands outside time, and therefore can be trusted to guide all time to the goal that he knows from eternity. This goal cannot be frustrated even by his rational creatures' turning away from his love. Catherine records God telling her, "It was with providence that I created you [i.e. humankind], and when I contemplated my creature in myself I fell in love with the beauty of my creation. It pleased me to create you in my image and likeness with great providence."[9]

---

[3] Julian of Norwich, *Showings*, trans. Edmund Colledge, O. S. A., and James Walsh, S. J. (New York: Paulist Press, 1978), p. 190.
[4] Ibid.
[5] Ibid.
[6] Ibid., p. 185.
[7] Catherine of Siena, *The Dialogue*, p. 325.
[8] Ibid., p. 326.
[9] Ibid., p. 277.

Providence, like goodness, wisdom and love, belongs to what is one in God. God's providence is the same as his love, wisdom, justice, mercy, omnipotence and other attributes of his unity. God is not a composite of diverse parts or attributes. We can speak truly about him by analogy from the finite perfections that he causes to be; but we cannot conceive of him *as he is*, since his infinite glory is infinitely greater than the truths that we speak about him. Catherine says, "You, eternal Trinity, are a deep sea: The more I enter you, the more I discover, and the more I discover, the more I seek you."[10]

In describing God's providence, Catherine observes that we can understand it in a Trinitarian manner. She follows Augustine's analogy for speaking about the three-and-one God. Inspired by the evangelist John's identification of the Son of God as the "Word" (*Logos*), Augustine reflected upon the "threeness" and "oneness" of mental activity. He considered our mind, our mind understanding itself, and our mind loving what it understands. These three are the same mind, and yet they are distinct like the Trinity. God tells Catherine that memory, understanding, and will were given to her in order that, through her soul, God's providence might guide her to himself. The Trinitarian image in her soul exists for the purpose of enabling her to share in the Father, Son, and Holy Spirit. Catherine characterizes God as saying to her (and through her to all of us), "I provided you with the gift of memory so that you might hold fast my benefits and be made a sharer in my own, the eternal Father's power. I gave you understanding so that in the wisdom of my only-begotten Son you might comprehend and know what I the eternal Father want, I who give you graces with such burning love."[11] God's providence works to lead us to the Trinity through our memory, understanding, and finally through our love. As God says to Catherine, "I gave you a will to love, making you a sharer in the Holy Spirit's mercy, so that you might love what your understanding sees and knows."[12]

When Catherine recognizes this triad, an image of the Trinity, in her created mind, she comments, "Then, when I considered myself in you, I saw that I am your image. You have gifted me with power from yourself, eternal Father, and my understanding with your

---

[10] Ibid., p. 364.
[11] Ibid., p. 277.
[12] Ibid.

wisdom—such wisdom as is proper to your only-begotten Son; and the Holy Spirit, who proceeds from you and your Son, has given me a will, and so I am able to love."[13] The power that God has given her is her soul or mind, from which flows understanding and will. Just as the mind generates understanding, so also, analogously, the Father generates his "only-begotten Son," who is the Word. When the mind understands something, it loves that thing insofar as the thing is good. Love proceeds from the mind and its understanding, since one has to know something in order to love it. As Love, the Holy Spirit proceeds from the Father and the Son.

But don't the processions described here make it impossible for God to be truly one? If there are two processions in God— the procession of the Word and the procession of the Holy Spirit (Love)—how does this not overthrow the divine oneness? Sticking with the analogy from the mind, the answer is first that the mind and the mind understanding (or the mind loving) are the *same* mind. There is a real unity: when the mind knows itself in its entirety, what the whole mind knows is none other than the whole mind. Second, we speak about God in two ways: with regard to substance, and with regard to relationship. When Jesus says "I and the Father are one" (Jn 10.30), the unity pertains to the divine substance. When he says "I do as the Father has commanded me, so that the world may know that I love the Father" (Jn 14.31), he speaks not about the one divine substance but about his relationship as the divine Son to the Father. The processions in God establish relationships: the relation of the Father to the Son (the Father's generation or begetting of the Word), and the relation of the Father and Son to the Holy Spirit (the Father and Son's spiration of the Holy Spirit). As constituted by relation to each other in God, the Father, Son, and Holy Spirit are distinct Persons (the relations are *toward* each other) who are the one God (the relations are *in* God).

Hildegard of Bingen interprets one of her visions as signifying the Father, Son, and Holy Spirit, one God. She describes the vision as follows: "Then I saw a bright light, and in this light the figure of a man the color of a sapphire, which was all blazing with a gentle glowing fire. And that bright light bathed the whole of the glowing fire, and the glowing fire bathed the bright light; and the bright light and the glowing fire poured over the whole human figure,

---

[13] Ibid., p. 365.

so that the three were one light in one power of potential."[14] The images in the vision pulse with energy, warmth, life, and love. The "bright light," Hildegard explains, signifies the Father. The Father is the personal source, the fount of the Godhead. Standing in the light of the Father is "the figure of a man the color of a sapphire." This "figure of a man" is the Son. Hildegard thereby underscores that the eternal Son, begotten from the Father, is from eternity ordained to become incarnate as Jesus Christ. Hildegard does not explain why the Son is "the color of a sapphire," namely blue. Since the "gentle glowing fire" signifies the Holy Spirit, perhaps the Son's blue color is intended as a contrast with the bright light (yellow) and the fire (red), so that the interwoven beauty of the whole is emphasized. The Son stands in the Father's light, and the Father's light also bathes the Holy Spirit's fire. In turn, the Holy Spirit's fire bathes the Father's light, and both the Father's light and the Holy Spirit's fire bathe the Son.

With the image of the Father, Hildegard associates truth and plenitude, "without any flaw of illusion, deficiency or deception."[15] With the image of the Son, she associates innocence and obedience, "without any flaw of obstinacy, envy or iniquity."[16] With the image of the Holy Spirit, she associates life and light, "without any flaw of aridity, mortality, and darkness."[17] In this way she seeks to illumine their distinct Personhood in the Trinity, without claiming that truth, innocence, and light are not possessed equally by all three divine Persons. She also connects the Father with justice, the Son with fulfillment, and the Holy Spirit with enlightenment. Truth accomplishes justice; obedience brings about the promised fulfillment; light inflames our hearts and minds. The three are interrelated and inseparable. Commenting on her observation that "the three were one light in one power of potential," she states that "this means that the Father, Who is Justice, is not without the Son or the Holy Spirit; and the Holy Spirit, Who kindles the hearts of the faithful, is not without the Father or the Son; and the Son, Who

---

[14] Hildegard of Bingen, *Scivias*, trans. Columba Hart and Jane Bishop (New York: Paulist Press, 1990), p. 161.

[15] Ibid.

[16] Ibid.

[17] Ibid.

is the plenitude of fruition, is not without the Father or the Holy Spirit."[18] Where one divine Person is present, so are the other two. Even though the Father, Son, and Holy Spirit are always present together, only the Son became incarnate. But the Incarnation did not thereby lack the presence of the Father and the Holy Spirit. It was by the Holy Spirit that the Son became incarnate; and the Son was sent by the Father into the world. In turn, the incarnate Son, Jesus Christ, "poured the true light into the world," since he poured forth the Holy Spirit upon his people.[19] The Holy Spirit leads us in Christ to the Father. The actions of the Father, Son, and Holy Spirit in the economy of salvation also reflect the personal properties that distinguish them in the Godhead. For example, the Son "was begotten of the Father in Divinity before time began, and then within time was incarnate in the world in Humanity."[20] The Son's eternal generation by the Father is reflected by the Son's temporal birth.

As we have seen, Hildegard sees "the figure of a man the color of a sapphire" in her vision of the divine Son, so as to place his Incarnation at the forefront. For the Father and the Holy Spirit, however, she sees a bright light and a glowing fire, respectively. In accord with the constant Christian understanding of God, therefore, she recognizes that the names "Father" and "Son"—which are proper names (rather than merely metaphorical ones) because they describe the reality of the Father's eternal generation of his Word— do not indicate that the Persons of the Trinity are male. The divine Persons, while infinitely personal, cannot be understood as either male or female. The risk of the images of light and fire is that such images could make the Father and Holy Spirit seem impersonal. In this regard, Hildegard emphasizes the personal activity of the Father, Son, and Holy Spirit: the Father has inexhaustible power, the Son became incarnate, and the Holy Spirit inflames our hearts and minds. The Holy Spirit drives out sin and unbelief, and the Son is the dwelling place of all who have faith because he can "be touched and known."[21] Both the Son and the Holy Spirit lead us to the otherwise unknowable Father.

---

[18] Ibid.
[19] Ibid.
[20] Ibid.
[21] Ibid., p. 163.

When the Son became incarnate, did the Son (or the Trinity) change? The answer is no. The Son is infinitely Son; any change in him could only make him less the Son (since he is already infinitely what he is). If he became less, he would no longer be the infinite Son. The Incarnation depends on the Son being fully the Son, rather than changing and becoming less. In the Incarnation, the Son unites a creature to himself in an unbreakable union; thus the change is on the side of the creature. Nor, as we noted above, can the unity of the Trinity be broken. One divine Person cannot break away from the other two. Hildegard remarks that "the unity of Their divinity is unbreakable; the Divinity cannot be rent asunder, for it remains inviolable without change."[22]

God's superabundant generosity is made plain when we know the Father, Son, and Holy Spirit. The Father eternally shares the divine being in begetting the Son; in creating us in the Word he pours forth a finite participation in his being; and he heals and deifies us through the missions of the Son and the Holy Spirit. God the Trinity, who is a divine communion in himself, makes rational creatures so that they can share in his divine communion. When we realize the extraordinary generosity of God, we can celebrate his extraordinary goodness and lovableness. Infinite goodness shares itself infinitely, and is infinitely lovable. Speaking in God's voice about the three divine Persons, Hildegard says that "for this reason I [God] have made Them known to Man, that he may burn more ardently in My love."[23]

Put another way, to love God, we need to know something about who he is. When he reveals himself to be Father, Son, and Holy Spirit, the generous outpouring of being that we see in creation and salvation makes sense. The temporal generosity is connected with the eternal generosity of the Father's begetting of the eternal Son. When God loves rational creatures into existence, he does so with the end or goal of supremely sharing his beatitude with us through deification. The possibility of deification depends on the Father's sending of the incarnate Son to the world and filling the incarnate Son with his Holy Spirit. At every step, we find that God's generous love knows no bounds. The inner generosity of God the Trinity shows us that his loving actions toward us are no aberration: they

---

[22] Ibid., p. 162.
[23] Ibid.

are rooted in God's own life. Only by knowing God as Trinity can we fully appreciate the infinite goodness of God, who shares himself entirely. In this way we "burn more ardently" in the love of God.

We could not know or love God in this way without his help. Hildegard quotes 1 John 4.9, "In this the love of God was made manifest among us, that God sent his only Son into the world, so that we might live through him."[24] She extols "the embrace of God's maternal love, which has nourished us unto life and is our help in perils."[25] God loves us into existence in creation, and loves us into a new and richer existence in Christ Jesus. God "has mercifully remembered His great work and His precious pearl, Man, whom He formed from the mud of the earth and into whom He breathed the breath of life."[26] Hildegard specifies that the Father, Son, and Holy Spirit retain their unity and eternity even in enabling creatures to relate to them in new ways. She states that "no misfortune or change can touch God," since otherwise Father would become less than (or different from) Father, Son less than Son, and Spirit less than Spirit.[27] When the Father, Son, and Holy Spirit change us, they do so as themselves, the eternal and unchanging God. It is precisely because they remain fully themselves that they can restore us and draw us into their life.

Hildegard likes to find "triads" in everyday things that exercise the mind's contemplation of the Trinity. When we touch a stone, for example, the stone is solid and is either cool or hot to the touch. She associates a stone's coolness with the Father's eternal power; a stone's solidity with the incarnate Son's ability to be touched; and a stone's hotness with the Holy Spirit's enkindling of our hearts and minds. The goal here is to help us appreciate our distinct relations with the three Persons of the one God. Unlike living things, which are prone to decay, a cool rock will last for ages. The Father is the rock of ages, eternal in power. The Son is like a rock that is solid to our touch. We can touch him, because he became incarnate. The Son is the cornerstone of the Church. Like a fiery rock that warms the air and that sheds light, the Holy Spirit makes us warm with the love of God and enlightens our minds with knowledge of God. Hildegard

---

[24] See ibid.
[25] Ibid.
[26] Ibid.
[27] Ibid.

also compares our relationship to the divine Persons to the different ways that a stone house can affect us. To try to understand the eternal and uncaused Father directly rather than through the Son and Spirit leads to the loss of faith and to spiritual illness, just as dwelling in a building of cool stones leads to bodily illness. When we base our faith on the solid rock of Christ, by contrast, we dwell secure. In this dwelling place, the warm stone of the Holy Spirit keeps us healthy by overcoming the chill of sin and unbelief.

Hildegard adopts the same approach with regard to the triad observable in a flame of fire: a flame has "brilliant light and red power and fiery heat."[28] The fiery heat is the Holy Spirit in the hearts of the faithful; the red power is the enduring salvific strength of the incarnate Son; the brilliant light is the Father to whom the Holy Spirit and the Son lead believers. The three aspects of the one flame help us to see why it is good that the one God is three Persons. Likewise, in the oral production of words, "there is sound, force and breath."[29] The breath is the sweetness of the Holy Spirit; the "force" or meaning is the divine Word, the Son; the sound is the "ineffable power" of the Father. Encountering the Trinity, we encounter the power, wisdom, and love of God, and the three are one: "the Father, Son and Holy Spirit are not divided from one another, but do Their works together."[30] When unfolded in this fashion, the unity of stone, flame, or word manifests a threeness: wherever the flame's brightness is, there too will be its power and heat, so that the Father, Son, and Holy Spirit act together even while acting in accord with the personal properties that make them distinct.

Since the Trinity does not divide the unity of God, we can rejoice that God comprises both personal unity and interpersonal communion. Hildegard repeatedly challenges the view that the three-and-one is impossible or undesirable. She criticizes those who claim that "God is so powerless that He cannot truly live in three Persons, but only exist weakly in one."[31] She urges us to embrace God the Trinity in love, because in his love the Father has created and redeemed us through the Son and Holy Spirit. It is fitting that the Father sent the Son, because the Son, who is the only-begotten

---

28 Ibid., p. 163.
29 Ibid., p. 164.
30 Ibid.
31 Ibid.

in God, is fittingly only-begotten in virginity. His temporal birth mirrors his eternal filiation. Where the Son is, there we find the Father and the Holy Spirit.

Julian of Norwich says that "there is no created being who can know how much and how sweetly and how tenderly the Creator loves us."[32] In knowing God the Father, Son, and Holy Spirit, we obtain a deeper appreciation for the source and depths of that love. Julian advises that we keep God's goodness always in mind in our prayer. God's goodness corresponds with his infinite generosity in sharing his being, both in his divine life and in his creative and redemptive love for us. In the same vein, Angela of Foligno reports an experience of ecstasy: "My soul has just been elevated to a state of joy so great that it is totally unspeakable. I cannot say anything about it. In this state I knew everything I wanted to know and possessed all I wanted to possess. I saw the All Good."[33] Angela goes on to explain the darkness of this knowing, a darkness caused by the fact that God is infinitely greater (brighter) than the light of our minds. Because the divine All Good "surpasses every good," Angela observes that "[a]ll else, in comparison, is but darkness."[34] Angela requires that we seek, in prayer, to know God not simply as an abstraction but "as he is in himself."[35] When we come to know God in this way, as the All Good, we enter into God in love rather than pondering him from the outside: "Discovering that God is good, the soul loves him for his goodness. Loving him, it desires to possess him; desiring him, it gives all that it has and can have, even its own self, in order to possess him; and in possessing him, the soul experiences and tastes his sweetness."[36] Thérèse of Lisieux similarly praises God as a "Furnace of Love" and an "Abyss of Love;"[37] while Maria Faustina Kowalska testifies in her diary that "God filled my soul with the interior light of a deeper knowledge of Him as

---

[32] Julian of Norwich, *Showings*, p. 186.

[33] Angela of Foligno, *Complete Works*, trans. Paul Lachance (New York: Paulist Press, 1993), p. 203.

[34] Ibid.

[35] Ibid., p. 300.

[36] Ibid., p. 301.

[37] Thérèse of Lisieux, *Story of a Soul: The Autobiography of St. Thérèse of Lisieux*, 3rd edn, trans. John Clarke, O.C.D. (Washington, D.C.: ICS Publications, 1996), p. 200.

Supreme Goodness and Supreme Beauty. I came to know how very much God loves me. Eternal is His love for me."[38]

Teresa Benedicta of the Cross (Edith Stein) can also assist us in knowing God, not least in her writings on St. John of the Cross's poetry. When God the Trinity enters our soul, we can think of his indwelling in the following manner: the Father is like the hand, the Son is like the touch, and the Holy Spirit is like the cauterizing agent. The Holy Spirit, who as Love is a consuming fire, "causes a wound full of delight."[39] When the Holy Spirit opens us up sufficiently, we feel love overflowing us so that it seems as though all is love; the sea of love is infinite and we find ourselves bursting with love, and yet we are not simply absorbed into the infinite sea but retain our particularity. The hand of the Father cauterizes us, inflames us with love, by the touch of the Son and the agency of the Holy Spirit. Regarding the delicate touch of the Son, Teresa Benedicta explains that our capacity to receive this touch, and the fullness of the Word's communication, increases in us so that our soul delights. She goes on to say (still following St. John of the Cross) that "[i]n the substantial union with God the soul recognizes the grandeurs and powers of all the *divine attributes* that are consolidated in God's simple divine being: his omnipotence, wisdom, goodness, mercy, and so on."[40] The perception of these divine attributes is like being filled with light, with each attribute wholly illumining the soul, but as though from one lamp. At the same time as we are illumined by the attribute, we recognize that we are seeing the attribute in shadow, as it were, because we cannot comprehend the infinite God.

Teresa Benedicta speaks also of how God prepares our spiritual faculties—memory, intellect, and will—for his indwelling. When we find that our memory, intellect, and will are stripped of cleaving to creatures, we discover how open they are to God. We discover how much God can fill them; indeed we learn that "[o]nly the infinite can fill them."[41] The faculties of our soul are like caves that we had imagined to be limited, but that turn out to be inexhaustibly

---

[38] Maria Faustina Kowalska, *Diary of Saint Maria Faustina Kowalska: Divine Mercy in My Soul*, trans. Adam and Danuta Pasicki et al., 3rd edn (Stockbridge, MA: Marian Press, 2007), p. 9.

[39] Edith Stein, *The Science of the Cross*, trans. Josephine Koeppel, O.C.D. (Washington, D.C.: ICS Publications, 2002), p. 196.

[40] Ibid., p. 203.

[41] Ibid., p. 206.

deep (though still finite). After our cleaving to creatures has been removed, but before God has entered, the longing of the soul for God contains an extraordinary suffering, an extraordinary emptiness caused by love's desire for union with the beloved God. Even to long for God, however, is already to possess God, though only through grace rather than through union. By grace, the soul longs for union. In this sense, to desire something other than God blocks the soul from recognizing the true object of desire. The soul focuses on the created thing and can no longer see the infinite divine riches, just as when something is placed in front of our physical eye so that we can no longer see all the other things that surround us. To love and praise God rightly occurs when we recognize that it is no mere duty, but rather it is the very delight for which we were created: the delight of rejoicing in infinite personal goodness.

In another work, Teresa Benedicta comments on Exodus 3.14, where God names himself "I am who I am." She observes that it is "highly significant that in the Scriptural text we do not read, 'I am *being*,' or 'I am *he who exists*,' but 'I am who *I am*.'"[42] In her view, the mysterious meaning of this name "I am" hardly allows for interpreting the name by using other words. Even so, she is willing to consider that God reveals himself here to be infinite, unrestricted "being," but only in the sense of "being in person."[43] The emphasis on God's personal existence is for her decisive. In order to be the Creator, God must have a fully personal, incommunicable, self-subsistent identity. As not simply "being" but personal being, God possesses infinite freedom and wisdom. Thus, Teresa Benedicta states, "The 'I am' means: I live, I know, I will, I love—and all this not in the manner of a successive or coordinated series of temporal *acts*, but in the perfect unity of the eternally *one* divine *act* in which all the diverse significations of *act*—actual being, living presence, perfect being, intellectual striving, free activity—absolutely coincide."[44] In the eternal divine act, supremely personal, there is no change because there is infinite plenitude; God "is all that which is."[45] Yet God is also the Creator of all finite being, all becoming:

---

[42] Edith Stein, *Finite and Eternal Being: An Attempt at an Ascent to the Meaning of Being*, trans. Kurt F. Reinhardt (Washington, D.C.: ICS Publications, 2002), p. 342.
[43] Ibid.
[44] Ibid., p. 345.
[45] Ibid., p. 344.

"nothing exists that is not called forth by God, that is not prefigured in him, and that is not sustained by him in being."[46]

Conclusion

To know the one God of Israel as Father, Son, and Holy Spirit places us before the infinitely personal mystery of his wisdom and love. As the All Good, he comprises both the infinite goodness of unity and the infinite goodness of personal communion. God the Father tells Catherine that because of the invisibility of infinite divine spirit, the Father sent the Son to make the Father's truth and love visible to us. It was fitting that the Father send the Son, rather than the other way around, because "my Son proceeds from me, not I from him."[47] The sending of the Son reveals both the Father and the Son, because "I am one with him, and he with me" (cf. Jn 10.30).[48] The purpose of this revelation is none other than to transform us by his powerful love and to draw us into the Trinitarian communion. Jesus Christ makes us the children and friends of the Father in the Holy Spirit. This relationship fills us with joy far, far more than can any merely creaturely relationship. We no longer live in fear of everlasting death; we learn that the meaning of the universe is eternal love and the fullness of friendship. We live this friendship now through the Holy Spirit, who fills our hearts with love and unites us to the love of Christ and his Father. God the Father explains to Catherine that at Pentecost (Acts 2), "the Holy Spirit did not come alone: He came with my power and with the wisdom of the Son who is one with me, and with his own (the Holy Spirit's) mercy, proceeding from me the Father and from the Son."[49]

Power, wisdom, and mercy: these characteristics belong to God in his unity, because no divine Person lacks any of them, but these characteristics also help us to understand the distinction of Persons in God. Power can be "appropriated" to the Father because it points to the Father's distinctive property as source of the whole Trinity; wisdom can be appropriated to the Word, who is eternally

---

[46] Ibid., p. 347.
[47] Catherine of Siena, *The Dialogue*, p. 117.
[48] Ibid.
[49] Ibid., p. 119.

begotten from the Father and in whom the whole Trinity (and all creation) is known; mercy can be appropriated to the Holy Spirit, who proceeds as love and gift. As lovers of God, we want to learn about the beloved God. In Christ and the Holy Spirit, we discover that the abundant generosity of the Father is intradivine and not simply aimed at creatures. We discover God as the "mad lover," filled with "immeasurable generosity."[50]

---

[50] Ibid., p. 325.

2

Jesus Christ

Who is Jesus? Gertrud the Great of Helfta says that Jesus' love for us is such that he would tell us: "Even now my heart is affected by such sweetness of love for you that if it were necessary for your salvation and you could not otherwise be saved, I would be willing to suffer now, for you alone, all that you could imagine I had ever suffered for the whole world."[1] When Jesus suffered on the Cross, he did so out of love for us, so as to heal from within the wound of our injustice by bearing himself the punishment due to our injustice. Through his path of love, his healing of the wound of injustice, we can truly be reconciled even to those who have hurt us most deeply, because we too are forgiven sinners. His love for us on the Cross is a divine wellspring of forgiveness. Even though we are sinners, even though we may be of little interest or value to others, Jesus loves us so much that he gladly gave his life for our healing and elevation to friendship with him.

In a mystical conversation with Jesus, Gertrud receives the insight that "a person ought carefully to wrap up all the troubles and anxieties of both her heart and body in his [Jesus'] own most holy Passion, like someone who inserts a twig in the middle of a bundle."[2] To join our small sufferings (our "twig") to the bundle that is Jesus' sufferings teaches us that suffering need not crush us. Suffering is our opportunity to learn to love, and thereby to overcome the fear and pride that afflict us. In our current state, we

---

[1] Gertrud the Great of Helfta, *The Herald of God's Loving-Kindness: Book Three*, trans. Alexandra Barratt (Kalamazoo, MI: Cistercian Publications, 1999), p. 137.
[2] Ibid., p. 139.

cannot learn to love without willingly enduring suffering out of love for others.

If Jesus were merely another human sufferer, however, he could not have suffered for the sin of the whole world, let alone for our sins. The unique power of his love for us comes from the reality that he is the divine Son, who became incarnate in the midst of his people Israel so as to fulfill the divine covenants and promises. This might seem a surprising thing for the divine Son to do, but Gertrud chalks it up to the immensity of the divine love for us. Jesus wants to lead us to the Father, Gertrud says, not just out of love for us but also in his human love for the Father. As the head of the whole people of God, Jesus shows "the uncontrollable nature of the most burning desire and love by which his heart was moved towards God the Father, for the salvation of the community."[3] Our relationship to Jesus requires us to seek to know his purposes, which are always rooted in love. Gertrud depicts this in terms of a vision of Jesus that she received during an illness. Jesus appears to her and offers health or sickness, for her to choose. In the vision, however, she "spurned both and, dashing between the Lord's hands in fervor of spirit, fled to that sweetest Heart in which she knew lay concealed abundance of all good, searching to know what was his most praiseworthy will."[4] Jesus calls us to come to him by sacrificing our selfish will, so as to gain our life by losing it in love for God and neighbor.

Jesus is our friend whom we know in faith now, and whom we will meet face-to-face after death. Recognizing that people sometimes suppose that Jesus is too great to have time to spare for lowly persons such as ourselves, Julian of Norwich observes how much we are honored and gratified when a great person publicly expresses care for us. "So it is," she says, "with our Lord Jesus and us, for truly it is the greatest possible joy . . . that he who is highest and mightiest, noblest and most honourable, is lowest and humblest, most familiar and courteous. And very and truly he will manifest to us all this marvellous joy when we shall see him."[5] The fullness of this meeting awaits the life to come. Julian anticipates this meeting with delight: "For the greatest abundance of joy which we shall have, as I see it, is this wonderful courtesy and familiarity

³ Ibid., p. 156.
⁴ Ibid., p. 163.
⁵ Julian of Norwich, *Showings*, p. 188–9.

of our Father, who is our Creator, in our Lord Jesus Christ, who is our brother and our saviour."[6] The graciousness of God's friendship with us awes Julian.

As a reward for her service to God in her youth, God gives Julian a foretaste of the heavenly life, the household of God in which we are fully included. In this mystical vision she "saw our Lord God as a lord in his own house, who has called all his friends to a splendid feast. Then I did not see him seated anywhere in his own house; but I saw him reign in his house as a king and fill it all full of joy and mirth, gladdening and consoling his dear friends with himself, very familiarly and courteously."[7] The Lord God mingles graciously among all his friends rather than holding himself aloof. He treats us as though we were his equals. We are truly his friends. Julian praises the "wonderful melody in endless love in his own fair blissful countenance, which glorious countenance fills all heaven full of the joy and bliss of divinity."[8] The presence of God among his friends is like beautiful music, a music that expresses endless love. This music and love emanate from his countenance. We see him face-to-face, and his face expresses the most glorious harmony, welcome, friendship, and love.

Indeed, Julian sees Jesus scorning the devil and other oppressors by treating them as nothing to worry about. What appear to be terribly powerful beings, to our eyes, are next to nothing in the eyes of God. When she sees how Jesus dismisses the devil as of no importance, Julian finds herself laughing. In her vision all of Jesus' friends laugh with her; it is the laughter that comes upon us when what seemed to be a terrible event has passed, and we are joyful and amazed that we were so fearful over nothing. Jesus does not laugh in her vision, but he deliberately makes her to laugh, "for I understood that we may laugh, to comfort ourselves and rejoice in God, because the devil is overcome."[9] She has a similar vision of Jesus on the Cross. At first his expression is one of profound pain and sorrow; he is on the verge of death. Then, at the instant of death, his expression changes to joy. When his expression changes to joy, she feels pure joy too. Joy is the primary reality, not suffering: "And

---

[6] Ibid., p. 189.
[7] Ibid., p. 203.
[8] Ibid.
[9] Ibid., p. 202.

then cheerfully our Lord suggested to my mind: Where is there now any instant of your pain or of your grief? And I was very joyful."[10] He suffered to make us sharers in his joy, and we must suffer with him in order to purge our selfish wills and enter into his joy. But the enduring, eternal reality is pure joy.

Joy is the truth of the world, although the fallen world is now being transformed through suffering. If we see the world right, we will see pure joy, pure love, peeking through. Right now we see Jesus in his suffering, but "[s]uddenly he will change his appearance for us, and we shall be with him in heaven."[11] Jesus' joy is so great that those who can see him, cannot help but become joyful. She says that "if he revealed to us now his countenance of joy, there is no pain on earth or anywhere else which could trouble us, but everything would be joy and bliss for us."[12]

Is Jesus' Cross thereby eclipsed for Julian? On the contrary. Jesus' shedding of his blood heals us. His blood washes our sins away, because in perfect love he restores the relationship of justice between us and God. She compares the blood that heals us spiritually with the water that sustains our bodily life. There is no shortage, no deficiency in the power of Jesus' blood. As she says, "The precious blood of our Lord Jesus Christ, as truly as it is most precious, so truly is it most plentiful . . . The precious plenty of his precious blood overflows all the earth, and it is ready to wash from their sins all creatures who are, have been and will be of good will."[13] The power of the Cross is present where Jesus is present. When he descended into hell, he "delivered all who were there and who belong to the court of heaven."[14] When he ascended to the right hand of the Father, where he now sits, his precious blood flows through him. Because his blood was poured out for our sins, his blood in his risen and ascended body makes intercession for all sinners, "and this is and will be so long as we have need."[15]

Julian describes Jesus' Passion in some detail. In a mystical vision, she "saw his sweet face as it were dry and bloodless with the pallor

[10] Ibid., p. 215.
[11] Ibid.
[12] Ibid.
[13] Ibid., p. 200.
[14] Ibid.
[15] Ibid.

of dying, and then deadly pale, languishing, and then the pallor turning blue and then the blue turning brown, as death took more hold upon his flesh."[16] She focuses our attention on Jesus' face, his countenance. She then describes the drying up of his flesh, as the blood and life left it. She associates the drying of his flesh with his thirst (John 19.28). She describes the crown of thorns and the damage that it does to Christ's head. Not only does Jesus enable her to see his Passion, but he also allows her to experience something of his pain: "in all this time that Christ was present to me, I felt no pain except for Christ's pains."[17] Her greatest pain, however, was to see her beloved Jesus in pain. Yet she points out that his pain was not one of despair; it was pain that leads to salvation, not the pain of the damned.

The purpose of seeing Jesus' Passion is to learn compassion, love that is truly for the other person rather than self-centered. To have compassion for another person is to be united in love with that person; rather than turning away in horror from the sufferer, we turn toward the sufferer in love. The Virgin Mary provides Julian with a model of compassion and so with the model of Christian discipleship. Compassionate love for the suffering Jesus leads us on the path to glory. As Julian says, "I chose Jesus by his grace to be my heaven in all this time of suffering and of sorrow. And that has taught me that I should always do so, to choose only Jesus to be my heaven, in well-being and in woe."[18] We must not turn away from the Cross, because it is by loving Jesus on the Cross and indeed by joining him there that we find heaven, which is supernatural love.

Jesus is one Person, the divine Son. The unity of his Personhood means that it is the Son who suffers. The Son suffers in his humanity, of course, not in his divinity. Yet Julian says that "the union in him of the divinity gave strength to his humanity to suffer more than all men could," not least because his humanity is most perfectly formed and therefore most sensitive both spiritually and physically.[19] A mere human being could not suffer the punishment due, in justice, to the sins of all humans. A mere human being would be unable to know and love each and every human, and therefore could

---

[16] Ibid., p. 206.
[17] Ibid., p. 209.
[18] Ibid., p. 212.
[19] Ibid., p. 213.

hardly suffer out of love for all. By contrast, Jesus could truly have compassion for each of us: "he suffered for the sins of every man who will be saved; and he saw and he sorrowed for every man's sorrow, desolation and anguish, in his compassion and love."[20]

Jesus freely loves us. Julian praises the divine generosity: "For it is God's will that we have true delight with him in our salvation, and in it he wants us to be greatly comforted and strengthened, and so joyfully he wishes our souls to be occupied with his grace. For we are his bliss, because he endlessly delights in us."[21] Julian never minimizes Jesus' suffering, but she observes that he has "the qualities of a cheerful giver," and "he always and endlessly rejoices" in what he did for our salvation on the Cross.[22] Only the incarnate Son suffers, but the Father and the Holy Spirit are also at work in Christ's Passion, namely by "administering abundant virtues and plentiful grace to us by him" and by rejoicing in Christ's deed.[23]

In mystical visions, Jesus shows Julian various marks of his great love. He shows her his wounded side, from which flowed blood and water (John 19.34), and he teaches her that the space of this wound is "large enough for all mankind that will be saved and will rest in peace and in love."[24] He shows her his heart, burst in half by his endless love. He encourages her with words: "See how I love you, as if he had said, my darling, behold and see your Lord, your God, who is your Creator and your endless joy; see your own brother, your saviour; my child, behold and see what delight and bliss I have in your salvation, and for my love rejoice with me."[25] In every way, Jesus' goal is to make us happy. He truly is our lover.

Jesus' love similarly characterizes Maria Faustina Kowalska's message about the risen Lord. As she is contemplating a beautiful lakeshore, she has a vision of Jesus, who says to her, "All this I created for you, my spouse; and know that all this beauty is nothing compared to what I have prepared for you in eternity."[26] Her defining vision of Jesus involved his giving her a message about his mercy. In this vision, she sees Jesus with rays of light emanating

---

[20] Ibid.
[21] Ibid., pp. 218–19.
[22] Ibid., p. 219.
[23] Ibid.
[24] Ibid., p. 220.
[25] Ibid., p. 221.
[26] Kowalska, *Diary*, p. 88.

from his heart, rays that spread from Jesus' heart through the whole world. The rays of light are actual physical light, witnessed by another person along with Maria Faustina. She later sees a vision of Jesus and Mary, and Jesus tells her: "I am King of Mercy."[27] He commands that the image of him with rays of mercy streaming from his heart be displayed every year on the first Sunday after Easter (as it now is), so that he can "make known the bottomless depth of My mercy."[28]

Thérèse of Lisieux, who upon receiving the Carmelite habit took the name "Sister Thérèse of the Child Jesus and the Holy Face," concentrates on Jesus' hiddenness and littleness, which we must imitate through *"surrender and gratitude."*[29] Contemplating the face of Jesus, she sees God's humility. Humility can be mistaken for timidity, but never by Thérèse. On the contrary, Jesus' humility is also an extraordinary divine boldness: he humbly comes to draw his creature into a bridal relationship with himself (cf. Rev 21.2), and he is "thirsty for love" (cf. Jn 19.28).[30] Thérèse's humility likewise manifests this boldness; she draws up a marriage announcement for "Jesus, King of kings, and Lord of lords, with little Thérèse Martin, now Princess and Lady of His Kingdoms of the Holy Childhood and the Passion, assigned to her in dowry by her Divine Spouse."[31] Her characteristic humor does not obscure the fact that she writes this marriage announcement in seriousness, because of her recognition that this is indeed how humble Jesus is. Jesus wills to marry us, his Bride, and to share his life of love with us, first in configuration to his Passion, then in configuration to his glory. Because of the need to overcome our disordered self-love, Thérèse comes to realize that *"suffering alone* gives birth to souls," as Jesus had promised when he said that the grain of wheat must fall to the ground before it can bear fruit;[32] not mere suffering, but suffering out of love for God and neighbor is what Jesus has in view. Thérèse longs to enter into the depths of Jesus' suffering and self-surrender, and she asks Jesus to unite her fully to "the fire of Your Divine Love!"[33]

---

[27] Ibid., p. 44.
[28] Ibid.
[29] Thérèse of Lisieux, *Story of a Soul*, p. 188.
[30] Ibid., p. 189.
[31] Ibid., p. 168.
[32] Ibid., p. 174.
[33] Ibid., p. 181.

The approach of Hildegard of Bingen complements these images of mercy and self-surrendering love. When Hildegard treats the Incarnation, she begins with the omnipotence of God, to which she joins God's incomprehensibility and fullness of life. As the omnipotent one, he is the Creator. Since he made us for himself, we long for him, and yet we freely rebel against him. For this reason God sent his Son, his Word, to take on flesh and redeem us. "In the course of time," says Hildegard, the Word became "incarnate in the ardor of charity, miraculously and without the stain or weight of sin, by the Holy Spirit's sweet freshness in the dawn of blessed virginity."[34] Jesus was miraculously conceived by the Holy Spirit in the womb of the Virgin Mary. He had no sin, and by his merits his mother was likewise blessed. Here we find a new dawn for the human race.

By being born of Mary, did the Word separate himself from the Father who eternally begets him? On the contrary, "after He assumed flesh, the Word also remained inseparably in the Father."[35] Miraculously, he is born without destroying Mary's virginal integrity or causing her pain; for Hildegard this symbolizes his unbreakable union with the Father in heaven, even while he is being born on earth. She also notes that he is called Word because through him, we come to know the power, holiness, and goodness of the Father. As a new dawn, Jesus' birth restored and invigorated human knowledge of God. She explains that we needed this restoration because although we were created in the Word, we turned away. God the Father "gave to Adam through His Word in the Holy Spirit the sweet precept of obedience, which in fresh fruitfulness hung upon the Word."[36] In his intelligence, Adam knew the law of God, but he did not savor God's law or fulfill it by his work. Instead he "sank into the gaping mouth of death, so that he did not seek God either by faith or by works."[37] He fell away from the knowledge of God. The Word came in the flesh to restore this true knowledge, so that humans could rise from "the horror of bursting and stinking sin."[38]

Hildegard roots the Incarnation of Jesus Christ in the covenantal history of God's work among his people Israel. She describes

---

[34] Hildegard of Bingen, *Scivias*, p. 151.
[35] Ibid.
[36] Ibid., p. 153.
[37] Ibid.
[38] Ibid.

Abraham, Isaac, and Jacob as "three great luminaries."[39] Like the holy Trinity, the great patriarchs of Israel are one with each other in holiness and related to each other. They spread the knowledge of the true God and they began to disperse the world's darkness. The prophets who followed them were similarly "radiant with many wonders."[40] She quotes Hosea 13.12-14, "The iniquity of Ephraim is bound up; his sin is hidden. The sorrows of a woman in labor shall come upon him; he is an unwise son; for now he shall not stand in the contrition of the sons. I will deliver them out of the hand of death, from death I will redeem them. I will be your death, O Death; I will be your destruction, O Hell!"[41] She takes this passage to refer to the conquest of death by Jesus Christ. The "unwise son" is the devil, whose rejection of God is complete and irreversible. The devil succeeded in tempting Adam and Eve, but the devil cannot conquer Jesus. Instead, Jesus fulfills the work of Israel's patriarchs and prophets by establishing true knowledge of God and obedience to God's will throughout the world. Jesus "sent out into the darkness of unbelief His clear and blessed teachings and salvation."[42] Rather than solely teaching by words, Jesus underwent his Passion and death for the sake of our salvation. In this way he conquered the devil and delivered his holy people from the realm of death. He "brought them back to the inheritance they had lost in Adam."[43]

Jesus' Passion overcomes the devil by suffering the punishment for our disobedience. Furthermore, Jesus delivers us "from slavery to idols; for idols are by their deceptiveness in the power of perdition, and for them the unfaithful forsake the honor of their Creator."[44] God's revelation of himself to the patriarchs and prophets, and Israel's condemnation of idolatry, come to completion in the true knowledge of God that Jesus brings, even though God remains incomprehensible because infinite. Hildegard's emphasis on Jesus as restoring our knowledge of God informs her image of the incarnate Word as "a great fountain, so that every faithful throat could drink

---

[39] Ibid.
[40] Ibid.
[41] Ibid., p. 155. The RSV version is somewhat different.
[42] Ibid., p. 154.
[43] Ibid.
[44] Ibid., p. 155.

and never more be dry" (cf. Jn 4.14; 7.37).[45] When the new day of Jesus dawned, Hildegard says, there appeared "the fruitfulness of the great and venerable counsel, so that all the forerunners marvelled at it with bright joy."[46]

The Incarnation of the Son and his victorious Cross should be received with joy; and indeed Hildegard associates these events with glorious music. At the Incarnation, "the angels suddenly trembled and sang the sweetest praises of rejoicing" (cf. Lk. 2.13-14).[47] The joy of the angels at the Incarnation is mirrored by the joy of the holy people of God when Jesus, having endured his Cross, descended triumphantly into the "hell" of the dead. The holy people had been waiting for Jesus' Passion to overcome original sin so that they could be fully united to God in perfect holiness. By his Cross, Jesus opened the gates of heaven. The holy dead thereby received their inheritance, namely the joy of dwelling with God as his children. Their streaming into heaven is depicted by Hildegard in a manner drawn from the descriptions of Moses' victory over Pharaoh and of David's triumphal entry with the Ark of the Covenant into Jerusalem. In Exodus 15.20, the people rejoice over their crossing of the Red Sea and the destruction of the Egyptian army: "Then Miriam, the prophetess, the sister of Aaron, took a timbrel in her hand; and all the women went out after her with timbrels and dancing." Similarly, in 2 Samuel 6.14-15 we read that "David danced before the Lord with all his might; and David was girded with a linen ephod. So David and all the house of Israel brought up the ark of the Lord with shouting, and with the sound of the horn." Along the same lines Hildegard suggests that after Jesus' victory, as the holy dead "were returning to their inheritance, timbrels and harps and all kinds of music burst forth, because Man, who had lain in perdition but now stood upright in blessedness, had been freed by heavenly power and escaped from death."[48]

The victory of Jesus over the devil—over sin and death—occurs by his shedding his blood. He entered the realm of death and despoiled it; death does not have the last word. Hildegard supposes that Jesus remained in death for three days so as to signify the Trinity; and it

---

[45] Ibid., p. 154.
[46] Ibid.
[47] Ibid.
[48] Ibid., pp. 154–5.

is the Trinity who raised the dead Jesus. She says that "the noble body of the Son of God . . . was touched by the glory of the Father, received the Spirit and rose again to serene immortality."[49] We cannot now conceive or imagine what his immortal life is like. We can, however, know that the saints and angels, in the glory of the Trinity, rejoice to see his victorious wounds (cf. Rev 5). We can also know what he brings about for his Church on earth. Above all, he gives salvific knowledge that enlightens us on the path to God: "[C]riminal forgetfulness of God was brought low, and human reason, which had lain prostrate under the Devil's persuasion, was uplifted to the knowledge of God; for the way to truth was shown to Man by the Supreme Beatitude, and in it he was led from death to life."[50] The risen Jesus also showed himself for 40 days to his disciples and to holy women who had followed him and who greatly desired to see him. He showed them his risen body in order to firmly establish their faith. After these 40 days, Jesus "ascended to the Father, Who with the Son and the Holy Spirit is the height of lofty and excelling joy and gladness unspeakable."[51]

Hildegard compares the 40 days that the risen Jesus spent with his disciples and the holy women before his Ascension, to the 40 years that the Israelites spent in the desert before they came into the Promised Land. The incarnate Son's ascending to the Father is the completion of the entrance of humans into the life of the Trinity. When we affirm that Jesus is both God and man, we affirm not a mere abstract truth but a salvific truth that expresses our destiny of sharing in the holiness and blessedness of the Trinitarian life. As the Son of God incarnate, seated in the flesh at the right hand of the Father, Jesus pours out the Holy Spirit upon his Church. Contemplating Jesus' Ascension and his pouring out of gifts to his Church, Hildegard says that "then indeed the new Bride of the Lamb was set up with many ornaments, for she had to be ornamented with every kind of virtue for the mighty struggle of all the faithful people, who are to fight against the crafty serpent."[52]

The doctrine of Christ and salvation that we find in Hildegard is furthered by Catherine of Siena's image of Christ as a bridge.

---

[49] Ibid., p. 156.
[50] Ibid.
[51] Ibid.
[52] Ibid., p. 157.

Speaking of a perfected soul, God the Father tells Catherine, "Open your mind's eye and watch her run across the bridge of the teaching of Christ crucified, who was your rule and way and teaching."[53] The bridge is ultimately the union of divinity and humanity in Jesus Christ. God explains to Catherine that the bridge is "my only-begotten Son" and that "it stretches from heaven to earth by reason of my having joined myself with your humanity, which I formed from the earth's clay."[54] By means of this bridge, those who follow its stairs can ascend through spiritual purification to union with God. The first step on the bridge leads the believer to contemplate "my Son's opened heart," where the believer "begins to feel the love of her own heart in his consummate and unspeakable love."[55] Since the bridge is Christ crucified, we encounter his outpouring of love and, warmed by the divine love for us, we are inspired to love him. This is the second stair, which involves us in a spiritual battle against the vices that prevent us from loving God and neighbor. Those who attain to the third stair enjoy the kiss of Christ's mouth and experience interior peace, a foretaste of the perfect peace of eternal life.

God tells Catherine that this bridge was erected when Jesus, without cutting off his divinity from his humanity, suffered on the Cross and rose from the dead. The unity of his divinity and humanity is crucial, because without this we would still be separated from God. God teaches Catherine that "though he was raised so high he was not raised off the earth. In fact, his divinity is kneaded into the clay of your humanity like one bread."[56] By submitting to the "anvil" of the Cross, Jesus bears the punishment of all crimes and reconciles us to God and to each other, and he does so freely out of love. It is this love that is the central element, because love draws us to him.

Catherine envisions the bridge as walled or covered to prevent travelers from getting wet. The "wall" of the bridge is virtue, and it protects us from the rain of injustice. This wall was fully formed only when Christ died on the Cross, because only then was the rain of injustice overcome so that we were no longer alienated

---

[53] Catherine of Siena, *The Dialogue*, p. 137.
[54] Ibid., p. 64.
[55] Ibid.
[56] Ibid., p. 65.

from God through our lack of holiness. Indeed, the stones of virtue "were hewn on the body of the Word."[57] The merciful building of the bridge's walls required "the strong heat of burning love," out of which the incarnate Son gave his blood for our redemption.[58]

The bridge takes us from earthly life to heavenly life, which we can already enjoy (even if not fully) while in our earthly lives. The bridge's gate would be locked if Christ had not shed his blood. Now that Christ's Cross has won our redemption, the bridge's gate stands wide open. The bridge and the gate are in fact the same: both are Jesus Christ, the merciful way, truth, and life (cf. Jn 14.6). Christ's humble truth destroys the proud lie by which the devil seduced Adam and Eve. God explains to Catherine, "That lie broke up the road to heaven, but Truth repaired it and walled it up with his blood."[59] God the Father adds that he is perfectly one with his Son, the bridge.

By contrast to the eternal peace to which the bridge and its gate direct us, the waters that flow under the bridge bring destruction upon humans. Indeed, when we do not attach ourselves to Christ's mercy, when we find ourselves repelled by his love, we do not stand in relationship to God. Rather, we remain in our unreconciled and alienated state, and we show this by our deeds. Only God can give us eternal life, happiness, and peace. When we cleave to the things of this world out of contempt for God, we do so foolishly, not least because they are passing away. The rushing waters under the bridge symbolize the onrushing passage of time and the drowning of souls who remain in their sins. The created things that we choose over God pass away, and we are left bereft of everything, cut off from our true happiness by our own choice.

Catherine explicitly relates the bridge not only to Christ's Cross but also to his Resurrection and Ascension. God tells Catherine, "When my only-begotten Son returned to me forty days after his resurrection, this bridge was raised high above the earth."[60] Jesus Christ now sits in the flesh at the right hand of the Father. Since Jesus has ascended, has the bridge ascended with him so that we no longer have access to it? God explains to Catherine that through

---

[57] Ibid., p. 66.
[58] Ibid.
[59] Ibid., p. 67.
[60] Ibid., p. 68.

the Holy Spirit, the virtuous way of the bridge has become even more accessible to us. He says that "first I made a bridge of my Son as he lived in your company. And though that living bridge has been taken from your sight, there remains the bridgeway of his teaching, which, as I told you, is held together by my power and my Son's wisdom and the mercy of the Holy Spirit."[61] As the teaching and example of the apostles and martyrs show, Christ the bridge is still powerfully with us, through the mission of the Holy Spirit and in the power of the Father. Jesus will return in the flesh at the end of time, and until that time he sustains "the mystic body of holy Church"[62] as she travels along the bridge despite the failings of those who claim association with her.

Conclusion

In Jesus, the Creator becomes the Redeemer. The superabundant generosity that we see in creation pours forth in redemption as well. The intra-Trinitarian goodness, love, and wisdom are the basis for God's free action on our behalf in Jesus Christ. We should understand the Incarnation as involving the entire Trinity: God the Father sends the Son, who becomes incarnate through the Holy Spirit. Jesus fulfills the work of God in Israel preeminently by leading us to true worship through true knowledge of God. We come to know this true knowledge—that the living God is a communion of Persons whose love and mercy is powerful and inexhaustible—through Jesus' love, enacted on the Cross. Jesus' Resurrection and Ascension show us what God will do for those who follow Jesus' path. Indeed, God, the "mad lover," is already calling us to share in his eternal love here and now. "You, eternal Trinity, are a deep sea: the more I enter you, the more I discover, and the more I discover, the more I seek you . . . Clothe, clothe me with yourself, eternal Truth, so that I may run the course of this mortal life in true obedience and in the light of most holy faith. With that light I sense my soul once again becoming drunk!"[63]

---

[61] Ibid., p. 70.
[62] Ibid., p. 69.
[63] Ibid., pp. 364, 366.

3

Creation and providence

Treating the doctrine of creation, Hildegard of Bingen observes that God made all things for his glory. In all created things, we find traces and images of God. She pays a good deal of attention to the creation of humans as comprised of soul and body. She praises God for his creation: "Almighty and Ineffable God, Who was before all ages and had no beginning and will not cease to be when all ages are ended, marvellously by His will created every creature and marvellously by His will set it in its place."[1] God created humans for the material universe and angels for the celestial realm. Angels and humans work together in glorifying God. Hildegard concludes, "For spirits blessed in the power of God make known in the heavenly places by indescribable sounds their great joy in the works of wonder that God perfects in His saints; by which the latter gloriously magnify God, seeking Him in the depth of sanctity and rejoicing in the joy of salvation."[2]

Less lofty, but equally penetrating, are the questions of Birgitta of Sweden regarding the created order. She perceives these questions in a vision, in which the questions seem to be asked of Christ by an unsettled but brilliant monk whom she knows. Among the many questions that her vision raises are the following: "Why did you give us bodily senses if we are not to move and live according to the feelings of the flesh?"; "Why have you given men and women sexual

---

[1] Hildegard of Bingen, *Scivias*, p. 139.
[2] Ibid., p. 143.

organs and the seed for intercourse if it may not be spilt according to the appetites of the flesh?";[3] "Why have you created worms which can harm and cannot profit?"; "Why have you created ferocious beasts that also harm human beings?";[4] "Why did you give the angels a spirit without flesh and the gift of being in heavenly joy, whereas to man you gave an earthen vessel and a spirit—and birth with wailing, life with labor, and death with sorrow?";[5] "Why do animals suffer inconveniences when they will not have eternal life and do not have the use of reason?"; "Why does a wicked man die a good death like the just; and the just sometimes a bad death like the unjust?"[6]

What response does Christ give to these questions in Birgitta's vision? The reason why we have bodily senses, feelings of the flesh, is so that we might choose the actions that lead to life and avoid actions that lead to death. The reason why we have sexual organs and desires is so that within the union of marriage, we might have children. Regarding God's creation of vile worms, Christ replies that he created "nothing without a reason and nothing without a similarity to spiritual things."[7] God permits vile worms to harm humans as a just punishment for sin. This is fitting because human pride thereby finds itself brought low by mere worms. In this condition, humans recall their utter dependence on God. Ferocious beasts serve a similar purpose. Christ notes that God at times permits ferocious beasts to harm even good persons, as part of God's providential testing of the good. Had Adam and Eve not sinned, however, the beasts would not have posed this threat to humans.

In answer to the question about why God created humans without the seeming advantages of the angels, Christ explains that "if man had a soul and no flesh, he would not be able to merit so sublime a good nor even be able to labor. The body was joined to the soul for the attainment of eternal honor."[8] When we suffer in the body, we are reminded not to be proud (as the fallen angels

---

[3] Birgitta of Sweden, *Life and Selected Revelations*, ed. Marguerite Tjader Harris, trans. Albert Ryle Kezel (New York: Paulist Press, 1990), p. 104.
[4] Ibid., p. 106.
[5] Ibid., p. 116.
[6] Ibid., p. 139.
[7] Ibid., p. 106.
[8] Ibid., p. 117.

were). Bodily suffering, as a sign of our approaching death, makes ridiculous our pride in our attainments. Furthermore, our bodily suffering enables us to yearn all the more for the eternal glory that God has promised us. Although we would not have suffered in this way had our human nature not been disordered by sin, nonetheless God makes good use of our bodily suffering and it assists us in our journey.

According to the answer that Christ gives in Birgitta's vision, the suffering of animals also has to do with the world's disorder. In a disordered creation, animals and humans are all too often enemies, each harming the other. Christ adds that "animals also sometimes suffer because of the intemperance of their own nature," given the fact that they are wild.[9] Because the suffering of animals has to do with the world's disorder, the salvation of the world by Christ should lead to less suffering on the part of animals. Specifically, for the sake of the Creator, humans should "be all the more gentle toward my creatures and animals."[10]

It might seem to impugn God's providence that the wicked sometimes experience a good death, while the just sometimes undergo a bad death. Christ answers that even the wicked can do some works of justice for which they merit reward in this life, and the good often do some works of injustice for which they merit punishment in this life. A contemptible death can be a providential reward for the just, by cleansing them from the need for any further purgation. Correspondingly, for the wicked a good death might be a providential punishment that dulls the conscience of the wicked at the moment of death. The point is that the operation of God's providence cannot be understood from exterior evidence.

Julian of Norwich has a vision of the created order as no bigger than a small round hazelnut. In the course of this vision, she realizes that creation, although it appears vast to us, is so little that it would immediately fall into nonexistence were it not for God's preserving it. When we recognize creation's littleness, says Julian, we can avoid the temptation to cleave to created things rather than to God. She writes that in reverence and humility, "a creature should see the Lord marvellously great, and herself marvellously little."[11] Even the

---

[9] Ibid., p. 140.
[10] Ibid.
[11] Julian of Norwich, *Showings*, p. 308.

smallest creature teaches us the marvel that is the Creator God. In comparison with God, we must despise "as nothing all things which are created," even ourselves.[12] Then we can truly know and love the Creator rather than focusing our love on created things.

Are we to imagine a big Creator who produces little creatures to stand alongside himself, like a big person holding a little hazelnut? Certainly not. Creatures do not add being to God who is infinite being. Rather, God's act of creation brings into existence things that share in a finite mode in his infinite being. As Julian boldly puts it, "I saw no difference between God and our substance, but, as it were, all God; and still my understanding accepted that our substance is in God, that is to say that God is God, and our substance is a creature in God."[13] Our substance does not stand on its own autonomously from God, as if we were competitors with God for existence. Instead we have substance precisely as creatures who receive finite being by God's act of sharing his being in finite modes. Julian conceives of the Creator as truth (father), wisdom (mother), and goodness (lord); and of course as Father, Son, and Holy Spirit.

Since God is eternal rather than temporal, God does not come to know us from a previous stage of not knowing us. In this regard Julian remarks that "I saw that God never began to love mankind; for just as mankind will be in endless bliss, fulfilling God's joy with regard to his works, just so has that same mankind been known and loved in God's prescience from without beginning in his righteous intent."[14] God's knowledge and love of us is eternal, because God is not temporal. From eternity, God knows and wills that we are to be. But creatures exist in time, and so it is true to say that God, in his transcendent knowledge and will, has always known and loved us even when in time we did not yet exist. Julian underscores that "just as we were to be without end, so we were treasured and hidden in God, known and loved from without beginning."[15]

Whereas God creates angels as spiritual creatures, he creates humans as unities of body and spirit (soul). God makes the human body out of the earth. By contrast, "man's soul is made of nothing,"[16]

---

[12] Ibid., p. 184.
[13] Ibid., p. 285.
[14] Ibid., p. 283.
[15] Ibid., p. 284.
[16] Ibid.

because God creates it directly rather than forming it from any preexisting substance. Since we have spiritual souls rather than being simply another animal, we are made for personal communion through knowing and loving. God makes us for communion with himself. As Julian says, "Our soul is created to be God's dwelling place, and the dwelling of our soul is God, who is uncreated."[17] God knows that this intimate union will come to be through the humanity of Jesus Christ. Our membership in the Body of Christ is so profound that we are caught up into Jesus' true Sonship as adopted sons: in this sense, says Julian, God "makes no distinction in love between the blessed soul of Christ and the least soul that will be saved."[18] In short, Julian distinguishes creation and Incarnation but does not divide the two in God's plan. Similarly Julian conceives of the soul as a "created trinity" marked by knowing and loving, as well as by mercy and grace.[19]

Julian ascribes three properties to creation: "The first is that God made it, the second is that God loves it, the third is that God preserves it."[20] God loves creation into existence. All creation bears the marks of the Creator; all natures come from him. Since humans have both material and spiritual nature, we are a microcosm of all creation. Julian states that "all natures which he has put separately in different creatures are all in man, wholly, in fulness and power, in beauty and in goodness, in kingliness and in nobility, in every manner of stateliness, preciousness and honour."[21] From this perspective, it will be evident that sin is profoundly unnatural, in the sense of being opposed to the goodness and flourishing of our nature.

God preserves creation so as to ensure that nothing in the created order happens by chance, "but all by God's prescient wisdom."[22] Had creation veered out of God's wise governance, then his power to preserve it (and to love it) would be in doubt. In this respect Julian differentiates between "the work of creatures," which can be ill done, and "the work of our Lord God in creatures," which always tends toward the goal for which God created, although we cannot

---

[17] Ibid., p. 285.
[18] Ibid.
[19] Ibid., p. 287.
[20] Ibid., p. 183.
[21] Ibid., p. 303.
[22] Ibid., p. 197.

always see how this is so.[23] Since God is at work in every created action, God "does everything" and from eternity guides all things "to their best conclusion."[24] Certainly we often do not recognize this. Since we cannot see beyond the present and do not understand the past, things seem often to happen by chance.

As Julian emphasizes, God does not do anything evil. Evil, as a lack of being, is foreseen but not caused by God, since God causes only being. God can use even our evil works to accomplish the ultimate good that he wills to achieve. Nothing that we can do can frustrate or change God's eternal purpose for the good of his creation. She affirms that God "never changed his purpose in any kind of thing, nor ever will eternally," because God knows and ordains everything from eternity, so that the good that he wills to achieve will not fail.[25] Sometimes in our eyes the world appears to be an utter mess, but God sees the good that he causes, and he knows the whole. Indeed, "the blessed Trinity is always wholly pleased with all its works."[26] God reassures Julian: "See, I am God. See, I am in all things. See, I do all things. See, I never remove my hands from my works, nor ever shall without end. See, I guide all things to the end that I ordain them for, before time began, with the same power and wisdom and love with which I made them; how should anything be amiss?"[27] The reason why God permits evil actions will be revealed in eternal life, but we can know already that it is an honorable reason that will redound to the credit of his wisdom, goodness, and mercy.

Could it be, however, that God takes care of one person but not of another? Or perhaps God cares for humans but not for other kinds of creatures? Neither of these views is true. God promises Julian that "every kind of thing will be well."[28] This promise holds both for the great and for the small. God will bring good even out of the evil deeds that cause so much harm. On the last day, God's consummation of all things will show us how he will make all things well. Does this mean, for example, that the demons will be saved?

---

[23] Ibid.
[24] Ibid.
[25] Ibid., p. 198.
[26] Ibid.
[27] Ibid., p. 199.
[28] Ibid., p. 231.

Julian accepts, as a truth of faith, that the answer is no. If some creatures are everlastingly condemned, then how can every kind of thing be well? Recognizing the problem, she says that God will not resolve it for our minds prior to the consummation of all things, when he will make everything clear. God reveals to her that "[w] hat is impossible to you is not impossible to me. I shall preserve my word in everything, and I shall make everything well."[29] God's act of consummation will make everything well, but in a way that does not contradict the truth about hell. Although she identifies God's gracious love for us as a deeper reality than is his judgment (because God's love for us is unchangeable, even though we may reject him), Julian warns against trying to unfold in advance the mystery of how all things will be well, and she also warns against denying that the devil will be everlastingly condemned. Instead we must focus on knowing and loving God, through the mysteries that Christ reveals to his Church. At the same time, we can rightly trust that even our sins will not frustrate the good work that God wills to do.

Much the same portrait appears in the writings of Catherine of Siena. Her characteristic note, however, consists in her emphasis on the constant care that God's providence offers us. She does not mince words about the failings of many Christians, especially the failings of many who have been elevated to the priesthood and whom God describes to Catherine as "my christs."[30] Repeatedly God bemoans to Catherine, in these or similar words, "How great is the stupidity of those who make themselves weak in spite of my strengthening, and put themselves into the devil's hands!"[31]

God emphasizes to Catherine that his providence can never rightly be blamed for our sins. It is true that we require God's help to do any action, because our very being comes from and is sustained by God. Since we do not have being in an autonomous fashion, we cannot act without God's assistance. God tells Catherine that "without me none of you can do anything."[32] In giving us being, God operates in our actions through what is proper to them rather than through the lack of being that distorts them; if an action lacks what is proper to it, this is our fault, not God's. God's providence

---

[29] Ibid., p. 233.
[30] Catherine of Siena, *The Dialogue*, p. 216.
[31] Ibid., p. 88.
[32] Ibid., p. 204.

never fails us. Catherine learns from God that "my providence will not fail you," nor will it ever fail any rational creature.[33] Although God does not fail us, nonetheless he allows us to freely turn away from him. He does not force us to trust his love. As God puts it, "I will not draw back from any creature who wants to come to me."[34]

Yet is not everything possible for God (cf. Mt. 19.26)? Why does it matter whether or not we want to come to God, given God's power to draw us? Catherine both explains why God does not compel us and prayerfully urges God to save us: "To you, eternal Father, everything is possible. Though you created us without our help, it is not your will to save us without our help. So I beg you to force their wills and dispose them to want what they do not want. I ask this of your infinite mercy."[35]

Does the extent of human suffering make folly of God's claim to be provident? When God permits us to suffer, Catherine emphasizes, it can be for our good. God tells her, "I send people troubles in this world so that they may know that their goal is not this life, and that these things are imperfect and passing."[36] Otherwise we tend to fall in love with this world and our own works, even if we began these works out of love for God. We can become stuck on "selfish sensual pleasure" rather than attaining the self-giving love that truly fulfills us.[37] When we are stuck in selfish sensuality, we turn inward rather than loving God and neighbor, and so we fall into pride, greed, and lust. We crave sensible goods in an insatiable manner, since we can find nothing temporal that satisfies our craving. We produce "fruit not of life but of death."[38] Catherine warns in particular against the "wind of prosperity" as potentially carrying us away in a fatal desire for worldly goods. Although prosperity is not evil in itself, it can produce "the wind of slavish fear," in which we live in constant fear of losing the temporal goods that we have.[39] In such a condition we can have no peace because we have cleaved to the creature over the Creator. As a "gentle doctor," God in due time allows us to lose

---

[33] Ibid.
[34] Ibid., p. 90.
[35] Ibid., p. 276.
[36] Ibid., p. 100.
[37] Ibid., p. 129.
[38] Ibid., p. 171.
[39] Ibid., p. 174.

temporal goods so as to defeat this slavish fear, but sometimes we refuse to release our grip on these temporal goods and we hate God because we have lost them.[40] In such cases, God remarks, "what I have given for life [i.e., temporal goods] becomes death to the receivers, with grief in proportion to their selfishness."[41]

Catherine employs the image of a tree at the bottom of which there is a thorn bush. This thorn bush is our difficult decision to take up our cross and follow Jesus rather than temporal pleasures. When we make this decision, we break through the thorn bush and the tree of God's "immeasurable tenderness" appears in its fullness.[42] Our free decision to follow Jesus is the providential purpose for which God gave us the power of knowledge and of free will. God created us in his image "with great providence," so that we "might be capable of understanding and enjoying me and rejoicing in my goodness by seeing me eternally."[43] God's providence for us includes his provision of Jesus, the incarnate Word, who redeems us by his holy obedience, by which he makes satisfaction for all sin. God's providence also includes the sacraments that unite us to Jesus' Cross and Resurrection so as to heal and nourish us on our journey toward God. The history of Israel and God's sending of the numerous prophets bear witness to God's providence.

Since God is the one who provides, we impede God's providence when we fall into presumption and trust in ourselves rather than in God. God does not thereby stop being provident for us, but we no longer recognize and embrace his providence. God explains to Catherine that "these souls certainly receive of my providence, but they do not understand it because they do not know it, and not knowing it they do not love it, and therefore they receive no fruit of grace from it."[44] When God permits them to endure even little sufferings, such persons complain against God as though he had abandoned them, when in fact they have abandoned him and no longer trust him. Our existential instability is not the fault of God's providence, since after all we have as our destiny not everlasting temporal life but everlasting life with God in the new

---

[40] Ibid., p. 175.
[41] Ibid.
[42] Ibid., p. 90.
[43] Ibid., p. 277.
[44] Ibid., p. 281.

creation. As creatures on a journey, we cannot remain stable. God's providence ensures that the universe in general and all his human creatures receive what is needed for the journey to the new creation. Especially for humans, these needs change throughout life. God says that "because none of you are stable in this life but are continually changing until you reach your final stable state, I am constantly providing for what you need at any given time."[45]

Yet does the evidence of human life truly support the claim that God is provident? Catherine notes that the death of the just is a major problem, especially when such deaths seem absurd and meaningless. We see the just "perishing now at sea, now in fire, now mangled by beasts, now physically killed when their houses collapse on top of them."[46] Of what providential use could it possibly be to have the just be crushed by a falling house or burned alive as a fire sweeps through a city?

Without the insight of faith, there is no good answer. The only answer comes from within a life of faith. The faith-filled person witnesses numerous instances of God providing for the good of people in ways that at first seem perplexing but later appear as works of providence. The great thing is not temporal life but rather is intimacy with God through love. When one sees that God provides in particular ways so that this great thing can increase, one learns to trust in God's providence for small things as well. Small things include all temporal goods. From this perspective of trust, gained from within the relationship with God that is faith, believers do not condemn God's "hidden judgments" by which God permits bad things to happen even to the just.[47] The spiritual senses required to rejoice in God's providence are lacking in those who presume to live by trusting in themselves. To appreciate God's providence in our lives and in the lives of others, we need to follow the way that he has providently given us, namely the way of Jesus Christ.

Catherine praises God's general providence for the universe, and not solely his providential care of humans. God makes and sustains the universe so that it continues in being and is good. Furthermore, he makes the universe so that it is hospitable to human life. Without air, fire, water, and the sun, humans could not exist. The same holds

---

[45] Ibid., p. 282.
[46] Ibid., p. 283.
[47] Ibid., p. 284.

for the usefulness to humans of plants, animals, fish, and birds. This hospitable world became less hospitable for humans after their fall into sin, but even so God's providential ordering remains apparent. The lack of hospitality that humans find in the natural world reflects the lack of hospitality apparent in our own souls when we have given in to selfish sensuality and lost all desire to return to our "homeland" in God.[48] God bemoans this situation: "My will they neither understand nor judge rightly, except when it seems to hold some worldly advantage or pleasure for them. But if this fails them, because it was there they had set their whole will and hope, they think they have neither felt nor received either my providence or any kindness."[49] At the same time, God continues to sustain the providential order of sunshine, rain, and so forth, demonstrating his universal providence as well as his providential care of humans. Catherine repeats that even when God permits us to suffer, he does so with providential care so as to prompt us to seek our eternal homeland.

For Catherine, then, the central thing to learn about God's providence is the following: "No matter where they turn, spiritually and materially they will find nothing but my deep burning charity and greatest, gentle, true, perfect providence."[50] We can only see this, however, if we recognize that the goal of providence is our salvation. If we recognize this goal, then we find ourselves relieved of temporal worries and we can let ourselves fall into "the abyss of my [God's] charity."[51] We will not regret trusting in God to be our provider. Released from selfish love, we will find ourselves nurtured by the Holy Spirit and given a foretaste of eternal life. In this condition, the soul "is not afraid that she will lack the lesser things because by the light of faith she is guaranteed the greater things."[52] God urges Catherine: "Fall in love, daughter, with my providence!"[53]

In the form of spiritual exercises, Juana Inés de la Cruz offers a series of Marian meditations on the seven days of creation. These meditations encourage us to think of God's work of creation in

---

[48] Ibid., p. 290.
[49] Ibid., p. 291.
[50] Ibid., p. 290.
[51] Ibid., p. 291.
[52] Ibid., p. 293.
[53] Ibid., p. 298.

light of his work of redemption. Juana begins with God's words on the first day, "Let there be light" (Gen. 1.3). Light is not only God's first creature but also symbolizes purity, and therefore points to the purest of mere creatures, the Virgin Mary. Juana has in view the Fall, by which creation is darkened, and she has in view God's answer to the Fall: Jesus, who enlightens creation and does so most fully in Mary, who is preserved from sin so as to be the Mother of her Redeemer. At the right hand of the Father, Jesus has his Church with him in the person of his mother, a pure light. Juana rejoices in the closeness of the mere creature to God. Speaking to Mary, she praises her as being "nearest to the faultless, inaccessible Light of the divine Essence," since Mary is the mother of "your Son and our Lord."[54]

On the second day God performed his second work: "God made the firmament and separated the waters which were under the firmament from the waters which were above the firmament" (Gen. 1.7). Juana considers that this separation can symbolize Mary's fullness of grace and separation from sin. Water is purifying, and Mary, as a pure instrument of her Son, is a "means of our purification and sanctification."[55] The stability of the firmament mirrors Mary's stability in grace. As the stars adorn the firmament, so too do the virtues adorn Mary. The third day occasioned God's third work: "Let the waters under the heavens be gathered together into one place, and let the dry land appear" (Gen. 1.9). On the dry land God made plants and trees. Juana compares the vast treasures of the sea and the gardens of the earth to Mary's virtues, and especially to her humility. On the fourth day God made the sun, moon, and stars, and Juana points out that the creature Mary, in her justice and wisdom, is more resplendent even than the sun. God created the birds and sea creatures on the fifth day. Here Juana thinks of the water dwellers as symbolizing Mary's purity and of the birds as symbolizing Mary's soaring contemplation and charity. The sixth day saw the creation of land animals and humans. Among mere humans, "[s]he alone was the one in whom the image and likeness

---

[54] Sor Juana Inés de la Cruz, *Selected Writings*, trans. Pamela Kirk Rappaport (New York: Paulist Press, 2005), p. 176.

[55] Ibid., p. 178.

of God, erased by the sin of our first father . . . was restored."[56]
Mary is the true creature precisely because of her unique grace as
the Mother of God, and she, far more than Adam and Eve, merits
"dominion" (Gen. 1.28) in love over all other creatures.

   In resting on the seventh day from his work of creation, God
invites our gratitude for his creation of creatures and especially of
Mary, the greatest of all mere creatures. Mary has received "the
highest privilege God could make and concede to a pure creature:
to elevate her to the incomprehensible dignity and grandeur of
becoming his mother."[57] Juana cannot think of creation without
thinking of the extraordinary gift of the Incarnation: "O mystery
of the Incarnation! O Incarnation of the Word! O union most
happy for us, that of God and humankind! O wedding celebrated
by the eternal king of his only begotten Son with human nature!
When will we be able to understand you? When will we be able
to reciprocate such a favor?"[58] The meaning of the creature only
becomes apparent when Mary receives the gift of bearing the Son of
God in her womb. Juana concludes her meditations by urging us to
become true creatures, the creatures we were meant to be, through
imitating Mary by receiving and conceiving Jesus in our souls.

Conclusion

Juana's Marian meditation on the creature as destined to be perfected
by grace and glory belongs with Hildegard's more philosophical reflections on the creation of angels and humans for the glory of God,
and with Birgitta's discussion of the questions that puzzle most people about creation and providence, such as why God created vile
worms that harm but do not seem to help anything. The extensive
theology of creation and providence offered by Julian, and Catherine's insistence that God continually helps and guides us, emphasize
the infinite goodness of the Creator God who loves us into existence and guides us toward the goal of union with himself. As Julian
puts it, "every kind of thing will be well,"[59] thanks to the consum-

---

[56] Ibid., p. 188.
[57] Ibid., p. 201.
[58] Ibid., p. 203.
[59] Julian of Norwich, *Showings*, p. 233.

mation of all things that God in his providence will accomplish.
In his extraordinary generosity as Creator of the vast diversity of
things, and in his generous love for his rational creatures, God not
only makes things well as Creator, but he will make them well as
providential Redeemer.

4

Sin

If sin were not serious, we would not need a Redeemer. Indeed the gravity of sin is apparent to all of us when others sin against us and against our loved ones. How could oppressors get away with doing such horrible things to their victims? The victims are lost to history, seemingly completely crushed, while the oppressors often rise to greater and greater prominence, wealth, and success. Where is justice?

In Jesus, who bears the punishment for all sins, justice and mercy meet. Yet God does not compel us to accept the love of Jesus Christ. After seeing a vision of the realm of the blessed, Elisabeth of Schönau has a vision of "the place and punishment of the impious."[1] The angel shows her a place of dense shadows, dense shadows. She does not recognize anyone, but she sees that they appear repulsive. The punishment they endure goes beyond all imagination. She describes a conversation that she has with the angel in the vision: "When I asked him who they were and if they could ever be liberated from there, he responded that they had brought death upon themselves and could never be liberated from that place."[2]

We can turn away from God's love and center ourselves on ourselves. In a prayer to God, Teresa of Avila bemoans the fact that "we forget Your words in the madness and sickness our evil deeds cause."[3] We become blind to God, and we allow love for earthly things to separate us from God. We cleave with all our strength to things that are passing away. The actions that we commit in

---

[1] Elisabeth of Schönau, *The Complete Works*, trans. Anne L. Clark (New York: Paulist Press, 2000), p. 107.

[2] Ibid.

this condition are unjust and harmful. Birgitta of Sweden gives the example of a duke who connived in his own brother's death and who led a dissolute life, without any concern for "the things that he has done to his neighbor."[4] Birgitta similarly receives instruction about the queen of Cyprus, who "should guide the people of her kingdom toward mutual concord and charity; and she should labor that justice and good morals be laudably maintained and that the community not be weighed down with unusual burdens."[5] Birgitta warns the citizens of Naples, in the name of Christ, against the purchase of slaves, many of whom are being forced into prostitution. Christ tells her that "this is extremely abominable and hateful to God and to me and also to the whole heavenly court."[6] She also warns the citizens of Naples against the use of magic by which people seek to be in control of their future rather than seeking the will of God.

Guided by God, Catherine of Siena warns priests against simony, the attempt to make a profit on the grace of the Holy Spirit. God tells her that "the three pillars of vice" are "impurity, bloated pride, and greed," all three of which are interrelated and founded on "selfish self-centeredness."[7] Impurity involves lust, falsehood, neglect of spiritual duties, impatience, and so forth. Greed makes a person love wealth above all things, by contrast to Jesus Christ who gave himself so generously. Wicked priests engage in simony in order to gain the wealth that they need to finance their pleasures or even to spend on the children that they have illicitly begotten. They lose interest in God or in the congregation of believers that God has entrusted to their care. Instead of using the Church's money in the service of the poor and the sick, they use the Church's money on frivolities such as keeping fine horses. At the root of greed is pride, which manifests itself as sensual love of one's own self and service of the world rather than of God. God warns Catherine that such people "think they have pleasures and riches and great dignity, but their poverty and wretchedness is great because they have not the

---

[3] Teresa of Avila, *The Collected Works of St. Teresa of Avila*, Vol. 1, trans. Kieran Kavanaugh, O. C. D., and Otilio Rodriguez, O. C. D. (Washington, D. C.: ICS Publications, 1976), pp. 380–1.

[4] Birgitta of Sweden, *Life and Selected Revelations*, p. 191.

[5] Ibid., p. 192.

[6] Ibid., p. 213.

[7] Catherine of Siena, *The Dialogue*, p. 244.

riches of virtue and have fallen from the heights of grace to the baseness of deadly sin."[8]

Catherine identifies other vices, including slavish fear, hatred of God, rash judgment, vilification of others, and presumption. She enumerates the seven deadly sins, with selfish love being the tree-trunk and the particular sins being the branches. She compares evil thoughts, words, and deeds to the flowers, leaves, and fruit of a bad tree. These vices have powerful results. Catherine speaks of slander and deceit as causing "revolutions, the ruin of cities, and many other evils."[9] On a peace-making mission to Florence in 1378, she herself was nearly murdered when trusted friends tricked her.[10] In the spiritual life, selfishness can manifest itself in insidious ways. When we seek things other than God, we will inevitably feel abandoned by God; thus for example we often seek spiritual consolations (feelings) rather than union with God. We can even refuse to help our neighbors because we don't want to interfere with our prayer regimen.

In her struggle against sin, Thérèse of Lisieux found it useful to try to perform what seem to be small acts of virtue. She struggles against excusing herself when falsely accused. She undertakes small acts of charity that, by their nature, do not receive thanks. When she seems in the eyes of her community to have acted through selfishness, she finds that this humiliation enables her to be no longer so judgmental of others. She fights what she calls a "glorious battle" against sin, a battle that on the surface seems very small: namely, she labors to overcome a natural dislike that she feels for one of the sisters.[11] She prays specially for this sister and renders her various services, to the point that the sister imagines that Thérèse felts a particular affinity for her. Thérèse comes to see that standing on her rights does not befit Christian perfection. When she finds herself too weak to resist a useless argument, she walks away and manages to avoid worsening the situation. She shows that the defeat of selfishness comes first and foremost through defeating the desire for earthly reward. Through detachment from the claims of the self, we can learn to seek God above all. We no longer seek human praise rather

---

[8] Ibid., p. 254.
[9] Ibid., p. 173.
[10] See ibid., p. 173 n. 21.
[11] Thérèse of Lisieux, *Story of a Soul*, p. 222.

than God himself. She experiences true joy when she finds herself no longer susceptible to human praise and instead "sees herself as she really is in God's eyes: a poor little thing, nothing at all."[12] The focus moves from her to God, and this is tremendously liberating.

The links between Thérèse's words about her own struggle to uproot selfish responses and Catherine's discussion of "selfish self-centeredness" should be evident. It is not so far a journey from losing the small battles that Thérèse describes to losing the big battles that Catherine describes. What makes sin especially powerful in our lives is that its roots go so deep and are often so hidden. The terrible harm that humans do to each other must therefore be combated not solely by confronting big sins, but also at the deepest interior levels.

Since sin goes deep, it will be difficult to root out and therefore penitential practices cannot be avoided. In this vein, Angela of Foligno describes the penitential steps that she herself followed. The first step is to recognize the extent of one's sinfulness and to fear everlasting alienation from God. The second step consists in confessing one's sins; yet Angela admits that originally she found herself too ashamed to make a full confession. Even when she did make a full confession, she did so more out of fear of God than out of love of God. After the third step that consists in the prescribed penance, the fourth step involves a deepening of our appreciation for God's mercy. Seeing how merciful God is, we begin to love God more and therefore to weep more deeply for what we have done in the past to alienate ourselves from God, who is so good. At this stage, having come to know God better, we are able to know ourselves better and thereby to recognize more clearly the extent to which selfishness dominates us. In later steps, Angela begs forgiveness of those she has wronged, asks for the prayers of the communion of saints, and comes to love Christ's Cross and to seek to imitate it by forgiving those who have wronged her.

Thérèse presents the path for overcoming sin as one that follows our normal channels; we must learn to love more purely, by focusing our love on God and others rather than on the claims of self. Angela, however, reminds us that breaking away from sin can be accompanied by manifestations that are strange in the

---

[12] Ibid., p. 206.

eyes of the world, given the deep roots that selfish love has in our hearts. She tells us that the "fire of the love of God in my heart became so intense that if I heard anyone speak about God I would scream."[13] She means this literally! The friar who wrote down her remembrances, and who was related to her by blood, found himself greatly ashamed when she visited the church of St. Francis in Assisi and began to scream ecstatically and uncontrollably at the doors of the church. But when she tells him her story, he understands much better. In the months before visiting the church of St. Francis, she had been giving away her property, and after her visit God enabled her to become completely poor. As she recalls, she had a vision of Christ just at the moment when, having reached the entrance of the church of St. Francis, she saw a stained-glass window of Christ holding St. Francis close. She heard Christ tell her, "Thus I will hold you closely to me and much more closely than can be observed with the eyes of the body. And now the time has come, sweet daughter, my temple, my delight, to fulfill my promise to you. I am about to leave you in the form of this consolation, but I will never leave you if you love me."[14] Hearing this, Angela saw something indescribable, yet of immense majesty, that she terms the "All Good."[15] As the voice and vision faded away, she says that she cried out repeatedly, "Love still unknown, why do you leave me?" but that because her voice was choked, her words sounded like a jumbled scream.[16]

The point is that conversion from sin can be so radical that it overturns our normal routine. After returning to her home, Angela lies prostrate in bed for eight days. Overcome by a sense of God's goodness, she is nearly unable to speak. Angela's conversion, however, is not thereby finished. She still finds herself frequently dealing with concerns about her past actions, which make her feel profoundly unworthy of God's love. She has further visionary experiences in which she hears Christ teaching her that the whole world is filled with his presence and that his power cannot be circumscribed. Whereas her experience of sin makes her wish to place limits upon his love, he refuses such limits. She learns from him that "everyone can love him. God does not require anything of

[13] Angela of Foligno, *Complete Works*, p. 131.
[14] Ibid., p. 141.
[15] Ibid., p. 142.
[16] Ibid.

the soul save love in return, for he himself loves it and he is the love of the soul."[17] Our weakness and limitations do not impede God's outpouring of love, so long as we repent of our selfishness and turn toward him to receive his love. Christ is "nothing but love."[18]

It is not guilt over sin that inspires the deeper stages of Angela's struggle with sin; rather, her struggle comes about because she sees how rooted selfishness is in us and how loving God is. A proper understanding of sin does not underestimate it but shows to us the path of liberation from it. Angela describes an experience of being entirely drawn into God for three days, so that she only thought of God. After these three days, she emerges from the experience and finds herself feeling depressed. At this time, she has another visionary experience in which she hears St. Bartholomew praising himself and her. This praise only deepens her depression, and she later discovers that the voice was a delusion. God comes to her and, in restoring her, shows her that only God can console her. God reveals his glorious power to her: in the whole creation she perceives "nothing except the presence of the power of God," and she cries out, "This world is pregnant with God!"[19] The very next instant she sees the extraordinary humility of God, in comparison with which her own humility seems like pride. She explains that "because I had understood the power of God and perceived now his deep humility, my soul was filled with wonder and esteemed itself to be nothing at all—indeed, saw in itself nothing except pride."[20] When in response she abases herself before God, he allows her to know that he has in fact made her worthy of an extraordinary grace. Far from abasing her, God fills her with joy and sweetness. When she undergoes a period of spiritual dryness and feels abandoned, he comes to her and assures her of his great love for her, a love that is in fact especially powerful when through trials he draws her close to Christ.

In prayer, Angela asks God, "Lord, why did you create man, and after you did, why did you allow us to sin? And why did you allow so much suffering to be inflicted upon you for our sins, when you could have just as well made it possible that without any of it we could be just the same as we are, be able to please you, and be

---

[17] Ibid., p. 153.
[18] Ibid., p. 154.
[19] Ibid., p. 170.
[20] Ibid.

endowed with as many virtues?"[21] It was not necessary for salvation that Adam and Eve sin. God did not need humans to sin in order to be able to unite humans to himself. God never needs our sin. So why did God permit humans to sin in the first place, when God could have poured out so much grace upon Adam and Eve as to uphold them against Satan's tempting?

Angela receives what she identifies as a standard answer: by overcoming our sin, God best reveals his goodness, and by allowing us to sin, he permits the weakness of the human condition to manifest itself rather than overpowering it by his grace. But she then receives a deeper penetration into her question about why God permitted sin. Namely, she finds that suddenly "my soul was drawn out of itself to perceive that the mystery of what I was asking had neither beginning nor end."[22] Only the infinite will of God accounts for why God permits and wills what he does. Angela recalls that "my soul was suddenly lifted up and illumined to see the indescribable power of God, as well as his will. From these visions I received a most complete and certain understanding of everything I had asked about. All former darkness immediately withdrew."[23]

What then is the answer to why God permitted sin, when he did not need to do so? Angela does not say. She knows that she has been given a gloriously bright and satisfying answer about God's plan for all of his creatures, and she is in a state of complete illumination and joy. But the answer that she receives in this state of illumination cannot be put into words except for to say that, "I fully understood that God could have done things otherwise, if he had so desired, nonetheless, knowing his power and goodness, I could not imagine any better way he could have made his power and goodness known to us, or a better way he could have made us assimilate them."[24] She enters into a condition of extraordinary peace in which she feels totally reconciled to and in love with what God wills for her and for all creatures. The love and justice of God appear to her so clearly that she could have embraced even a verdict of her own damnation. Yet this state of peace is only a preliminary: God lifts her up still further and she sees, with ecstatic joy and without knowing whether

---

[21] Ibid., p. 177.
[22] Ibid.
[23] Ibid.
[24] Ibid., p. 178.

she was in the body or out of it, "something stable, firm, and so indescribable that I can say nothing about it save that it was the All Good."[25] The goodness of God, an infinite goodness that can only be tasted to be truly known, is the answer (beyond the capacity of any words) to her question about why God permitted sin.

Julian of Norwich offers an image for original sin that may be helpful here. She describes a vision of a lord and a servant. The servant—Adam—begins with an attitude of eagerness to do his lord's will, but as he goes off to do this, he runs too quickly and falls into a valley. Julian observes that he "is greatly injured; and then he groans and moans and tosses about and writhes, but he cannot rise or help himself in any way."[26] This describes the situation of Adam and Eve, fallen into sin. Human nature is so disordered that it cannot restore the union with the Lord that it enjoyed at the beginning. Humans now find themselves in the dark valley of death. The greatest agony for the fallen servant, says Julian, is that "he could not turn his face to look on his loving lord, who was very close to him, in whom is all consolation."[27] Instead of being able to gaze upon God, fallen humans have focused their attention on themselves and on the sensible creatures that they perceive around them. This causes fallen humans great pain because these things are passing away, and so suffering and death seem all-encompassing. The tragic thing is that God is present and seems absent only because we have turned our face away from him due to the alienation caused by sin.

Julian envisions fallen Adam and his descendents as suffering in seven distinct ways. First, our nature has been wounded; second, our body is now clumsy; third, our body is weak; fourth, our mind no longer sees clearly; fifth, we cannot rise from sin; sixth, we are profoundly alone, without the possibility of human help; seventh, we find ourselves in a narrow, constricted, and sorrowful existence. But as Julian sees the fallen servant in this condition, she is also surprised to see the fallen servant suffering meekly and not being blamed by the lord. Indeed, the lord makes clear that "the only cause of his falling was his good will and his great desire."[28] The lord expresses his intent to reward his servant greatly. If the servant

---

[25] Ibid.
[26] Julian of Norwich, *Showings*, p. 267.
[27] Ibid.
[28] Ibid., p. 268.

is filled with goodwill, that is, with charity, and if the servant has merited a great reward, then perhaps Adam never truly sinned?

The true meaning of this vision then becomes clear to Julian. She is seeing, at the same time, the old Adam and the new Adam (Jesus Christ). She does not see original sin without seeing its remedy; even original sin reveals the extraordinary graciousness and generosity of God the Trinity. The reward that God gives to the new Adam for suffering the punishment owed to the old Adam far exceeds what Adam could have deserved prior to his fall. God permits sin so as to show an ever greater graciousness. God finds, as Julian puts it, "that his great goodness and his own honour require that his beloved servant, whom he loved so much, should be highly and blessedly rewarded forever, above what he would have been if he had not fallen, yes, and so much that his falling and all the woe that he received from it will be turned into high, surpassing honour and endless bliss."[29] Through the Incarnation of the Son and his Cross, God brings extraordinary good from the evil of the fall and its woeful consequences.

Yet is redemption truly worth the sin and suffering? Julian notes that it takes her almost twenty years to understand her vision with an appropriate depth. At the end of this time, God instructs her that he showed her all men in Adam because "in the sight of God all men are one man, and one man is all men."[30] All humans are in the old Adam, and likewise all humans are in the new Adam. The point is that God loves us all as he loves Jesus Christ. God comforts and helps us; he always looks upon us with love, mercy, and grace. His purpose is to give us a share in his joy and bliss. In her vision Julian sees that God's love never falters. His gaze of love upon his creature, even and especially when Adam fell, astounds her with its power and beauty. God's gaze never solely has mercy; rather it always also (and predominantly) has bliss. The bliss comes because when God looks upon fallen Adam in mercy, he sees with bliss the new Adam, Jesus, who "falls" or suffers out of love. With steadfast love, God accomplishes his purpose of deifying his human creatures.

Julian also sees Jesus in the work clothes of a gardener; his task consists in tilling the soil until he has prepared a banquet for the lord, whom Julian recognizes as being filled with infinite love. The

---

[29] Ibid., p. 269.
[30] Ibid., p. 270.

lord is the Father, the servant the Son, and the love the Holy Spirit. She goes so far as to say that "[w]hen Adam fell, God's Son fell; because of the true union which was made in heaven, God's Son could not be separated from Adam, for by Adam I understand all mankind."[31] Certainly the Son does not fall into sin, but he does fall "into the valley of the womb of the maiden who was the fairest daughter of Adam."[32] Sin and suffering, in other words, never stand alone in the eyes of God. Rather they always stand in union with Jesus Christ so that they are never meaningless, as they would be without him. The Son takes on the work clothes of the old Adam, by which are signified the poverty, weakness, and mortality of fallen human flesh. He takes on himself the punishment due in the flesh to fallen Adam. The Father does not spare the Son, but allows him freely to suffer out of love for us.

Risen and ascended to the Father, Jesus now "does not stand before the Father as a servant before the lord, pitifully clothed, partly naked, but he stands immediately before the Father, richly clothed in joyful amplitude, with a rich and precious crown upon his head."[33] His crown symbolizes all the saved, and so when God sees and loves fallen Adam, he sees this crown which the incarnate Son merited by his Cross. This crown is forever "the Father's joy, the Son's honour, the Holy Spirit's delight, and endless marvellous bliss to all who are in heaven."[34] Nor is Jesus alone even now at the right hand of the Father. Already his bride the Church is with him.

Our sins and sufferings, then, appear differently when looked at from this Christ-centered perspective. Julian considers that life has in it two aspects. She states, "During our lifetime here we have in us a marvellous mixture of both well-being and woe. We have in us our risen Lord Jesus Christ, and we have in us the wretchedness and harm of Adam's falling."[35] Although at times our wretchedness makes us almost unwilling to accept comfort, if we endure patiently God will show us the presence of his mercy and grace in us. We are sinners, and yet we are redeemed by Christ's blood. We endure earthly suffering, and yet we share already in the life of the risen

---

[31] Ibid., p. 274.
[32] Ibid., p. 275.
[33] Ibid., p. 278.
[34] Ibid.
[35] Ibid., p. 279.

Christ by the grace of the Holy Spirit. Julian finds that Christ is in us in three ways. First, the risen Christ in heaven is with us because he already draws us to be with him. Second, Christ leads us on earth, as head of the Church. Third, Christ dwells and reigns in our soul. The hurt caused by Adam's fall is never without the help—the extraordinary help—of Christ's sharing in and overcoming this fall. The Son "greatly rejoices in his falling" because of "the raising on high and the fulness of bliss which mankind has come to, exceeding what we should have if he hand not fallen."[36] Into the pit of suffering caused by sin, Christ pours his glorious love. As a result, even though we remain sinners, we receive the grace necessary to avoid sins that would lead to our spiritual death.

Julian sums up her perspective on sin by observing that "God sees one way and man sees another way. For it is for man meekly to accuse himself, and it is for our Lord God's own goodness courteously to excuse man."[37] We must hate our sins, repent of them, and strive not to sin, because sin alienates us from God, who is our bliss. Yet we should not imagine that when God looks at us, he sees the same sinners whom we see. He looks at us with his love, and in his mercy he sees our sins forgiven in Jesus Christ, who sits at his right hand and who has lovingly and freely borne the punishment due to sin. He sees us as he intends us to be, as sharers in his glory. This becomes apparent already in the case of Adam, whom the Church identifies as a saint united everlastingly to God. Adam's fall was not the end of the story. By the grace of the Holy Spirit, God cared for him and redeemed him in Jesus Christ. Love, not sin, has the last word.

Lastly, we might attend to Hildegard of Bingen. She begins with the sin of the angels. Why did some of the angels turn away from God? She supposes that Satan "was so great at the moment of his creation that he felt no defect either in his beauty or in his strength."[38] In short, he wished to be God, to shine as God shines. The result was that his beauty was destroyed, because he was beautiful precisely as God's creature filled with the Holy Spirit. By turning away from God's infinite goodness, Satan and his followers "are outcast from all good, not because they did not know it, but because in their

---

[36] Ibid., p. 280.
[37] Ibid., p. 281.
[38] Hildegard of Bingen, *Scivias*, p. 74.

great pride they despised it."[39] The fundamental impulse of sin is to will to be not a creature but a God who is in control. Since God is goodness, love, and humility, the attempt to seize God-like power is itself a radical alienation from God. Satan and his followers find themselves frustrated and suffering because they want to be what they cannot be, and because they have rejected God even while knowing what they were rejecting. They have locked themselves in "the prison of Hell."[40]

Hildegard urges us to avoid this fate. Satan, certainly, tempted the first man and woman to disobey God, and they did so. Satan tempted Eve who then persuaded Adam. Hildegard points out that Adam could have hated Eve for this; and indeed, when confronted by God, Adam quickly blamed Eve for his own free action. Yet Adam did not persist in hate. He instead obeyed God's plan, the intention of God in giving him a wife. He did not renounce God's plan for marriage or for the continuation of the human race. In Hildegard's view, Adam and Eve shared a perfect love, because after their sin they returned to God and accepted his plan. She states, "For Adam could have blamed his wife because by her advice she brought him death, but nonetheless he did not dismiss her as long as he lived in this world, because he knew she had been given to him by divine power."[41] The permanence of the marriage of Adam and Eve during their lifetimes shows that God's grace was leading them out of the disorder of original sin, even though that disorder would afflict all generations.

Hildegard accepts that after original sin, Adam and Eve no longer had dominion on earth but instead found the natural environment to be a difficult and dangerous place to live. She envisions Paradise, Eden, as a place of immense beauty and peace. The question, then, is why God permitted Adam and Eve ever to sin. Why not preserve them in Paradise rather than allow them to subject themselves to misery? Why even give humans the ability to sin? She answers that humans, as the image and likeness of God, had to be put to the test. They had to exercise their powers of knowing and loving in a way that subjected them to the possibility of loving the wrong thing, the possibility of failure. This testing continues today. Human life is a

[39] Ibid., p. 75.
[40] Ibid.
[41] Ibid., p. 78.

continual trial that proves and refines our charity, just as gold is tested by fire and just as precious stones are polished. When we sin against God's love, furthermore, we cannot turn around and blame God for allowing us to do so. The act of injustice was committed by us, not by God. We are in no position to claim "to be wiser than God."[42]

Hildegard adds that the radiance of eternal life, where humans shine in God and God in humans due to the Incarnation, is far greater than would have been the case had humans never sinned and God not become incarnate for our salvation. She explains this enhanced radiance this way: "For when a field with great labor is cultivated, it brings forth much fruit, and the same is shown in the human race, for after humanity's ruin many virtues arose to raise it up again."[43] In conquering Satan not by power but by humility and love, God ensured that pride was crushed, humankind rescued, and all believers armed with the means to have everlasting life.

Conclusion

What then can we say about sin? Its depth does not go underestimated by the theologians we have discussed. They follow it to its roots, and they recognize how difficult it is to turn from it. They warn those who are acting in sinful ways, whether by enslaving women for prostitution, by simony, or by committing other unjust acts. They call the whole Church to holiness. They recognize that sin has plagued the human race since the beginning—or nearly the beginning—and they understand that the history of human suffering reflects the terrible power of sin. Nonetheless they refuse to see sin in any light other than Jesus Christ, who reveals and embodies the love and mercy of God. In mourning sin, they rejoice in salvation.

---

[42] Ibid., p. 87.
[43] Ibid., p. 88.

5

Sacraments

Since the sacraments govern the rhythm of our journey through life, it is fitting to begin this chapter with the pilgrimage to the Holy Land that Egeria made in the early fifth century. Her diary opens with what she believes to be Mount Sinai in sight. Hiking to the top of the mountain with a group of monks and a priest, she finds a church at the top of the mountain, with numerous priests and monks from the surrounding area gathered to celebrate the Eucharist. She describes the scene: "All of the proper passage from the Book of Moses was read, the sacrifice was offered in the prescribed manner, and we received Communion."[1] After Mass, she views the places where Moses was thought to have been, and from the mountain she is able to see the lands of Egypt and Palestine. She journeys on to the place where Elijah resided on Mount Horeb and again shares in the sacrifice of the Eucharist. The location of the burning bush was also a tourist site at this time, and the priests celebrated the Eucharist there for Egeria's group. She describes in detail the liturgical practice in Jerusalem during Holy Week. Her journey is centered around the biblical mysteries, and thus around the sacraments by which we participate in these mysteries.

It is not so large a step, therefore, from Egeria to the autobiographical writings of Thérèse of Lisieux and others: despite the difference in times, the sacraments possess the same central role. Thérèse speaks of her first communion, her first reception of the Eucharist: "Ah! how sweet was that first kiss of Jesus! It was a

---

[1] Egeria, *Egeria: Diary of a Pilgrimage*, trans. George E. Gingras (New York: Newman Press, 1970), p. 52.

kiss of *love*; I *felt* that *I was loved*, and I said: 'I love You, and I give myself to You forever!'"[2] She thinks of the Eucharist in nuptial terms, in a manner that fits with Egeria's sustaining her pilgrimage through the celebration of the Eucharist. Thérèse understands the sacrament of confirmation also as an embrace of the divine love, in this case through a particular relationship with the Holy Spirit who comes to her in the sacrament so as to enable her to suffer with Christ. In the sacrament of marriage, Birgitta of Sweden prays for her husband's soul and she goes on pilgrimage with him to San Diego de Compostella in Spain.[3] Gertrud the Great, who lived in a convent that was for a short while under an interdict (when the Eucharist could not be celebrated there), repeatedly has visions and conversations with the Lord that are related to the reception of the Eucharist. Catherine of Siena devotes much of her effort to urging the priests of her day to live holier lives, since the pleasure- and power-seeking way in which many of them were living had become a scandal. All these theologians place the sacraments at the center of their vocation.

Let me begin by concentrating on the sacramental theology of Hildegard of Bingen. Hildegard notes that the Church "bears her children by regeneration in the Spirit and in water."[4] Baptism is not a guarantee of a holy life. Many of those who are baptized and become her children will depart from Christ through deadly sins, and will be condemned if they do not repent. In baptism (including infant baptism), the Church gives birth to children in a manner analogous to how the Virgin Mary miraculously gave birth to Jesus Christ. Hildegard characterizes baptism as "the sacred anointing of the Holy Spirit, because the person is renewed by the true circumcision of the Spirit and water, and thus offered to the Supreme Beatitude Who is the Head of all, and made a member of Christ, regenerated unto salvation by invocation of the Holy Trinity."[5] The baptized are enabled to offer true worship to God the Trinity.

Baptism forgives our sins by the power of Christ and the grace of the Holy Spirit. As the fulfillment of the sacrament of circumcision, baptism welcomes both male and female into the people of God.

---

[2] Thérèse of Lisieux, *Story of a Soul*, p. 77.
[3] Birgitta of Sweden, *Life and Selected Revelations*, p. 77.
[4] Hildegard of Bingen, *Scivias*, p. 170.
[5] Ibid., p. 173.

Baptism provides us with the armor of God so that we can defend ourselves against vice and be strong in virtue. Through baptism Christ forgives all our sins and sanctifies us, even when this baptism is administered by a sinful priest. In infant baptism, Mother Church offers her faith in lieu of the infant's faith, but personal faith remains necessary if the baptized wish to receive the sanctifying grace of baptism when they come of age. No matter who performs the baptism, it is valid so long as the Father, Son, and Holy Spirit are invoked.

The sacrament of confirmation follows that of baptism. Hildegard links confirmation with the descent of the Holy Spirit at Pentecost. At Pentecost, she says, "the new Bride of the Lamb was adorned and confirmed in the fire of the ardor of the Holy Spirit for the perfection of her beauty."[6] Prior to Pentecost, the apostles had received baptism but lacked the courage to preach and suffer for the Gospel. The descent of the Holy Spirit at Pentecost changed them so that "they were so confirmed that they did not shrink from any penalty, but bravely endured it."[7] Just as the apostolic Church was confirmed by the gift of the Holy Spirit, so, too, the Holy Spirit strengthens the baptized through sacrament of confirmation. The bishops, as the successors of the apostles, confer this sacrament. Confirmation sanctifies the baptized by enkindling the virtues and pouring forth all the gifts of the Holy Spirit. Confirmation enables us to boldly proclaim faith in the Trinity. The Church asks confirmation for her baptized children so that they too might exhibit the courage that the apostles showed after Pentecost. Regeneration and the forgiveness of sins belong to baptism, while adornment "with the shining gifts of the Holy Spirit by their anointing with chrism given to those baptized in faith by the hand of the bishop" belongs to confirmation.[8] Born anew by baptism, the faithful remain weak and need the strengthening grace of confirmation. In Hildegard's vision, God compares the combination of baptism and confirmation to the apostles' situation: "Love of My Son was secretly burning in their minds, and thus the fire of the Holy Spirit passed through them and showed the bright sunlight of their teaching."[9]

---

[6] Ibid., pp. 189–90.
[7] Ibid., p. 190.
[8] Ibid., p. 192.
[9] Ibid., p. 193.

Hildegard admits the ability of baptized and confirmed persons to fall away from Christ. Despite the power of the Holy Spirit at work in these sacraments, humans can still turn away. If even the angels could fall from grace, no wonder that humans can; God does not force us to love him. Some of those who are baptized and confirmed follow Jesus with undivided minds and hearts; others seek eternal life and truly believe but give way to some venial vices; others undergo powerful temptations and foolishly make more a show than a reality of Christian faith; others do not follow God's law but instead "fix their minds on earthly things more than heavenly;" still others go so far as to attack the faith and moral law of the Church. Yet for those who abandon and even attack the Church, the penitential path of repentance remains open for salvation.

Hildegard sees the Church as joined to Christ and nourished by him through the power of his Passion, his spilling of his blood on the Cross. Christ the bridegroom gives his bride the Church the dowry of his body and blood. In turn, the Church "devotedly offers her dowry, which is the body and blood of the Son of God, to the Creator of all in humble obedience," in the presence of the angels.[10] This offering is the Eucharist. The priest offers Christ's body and blood under the signs of bread and wine, which Christ used at the Last Supper to symbolize the offering that he was to make on the Cross. The eucharistic elements must therefore be wheaten bread and grape wine mixed with water. The Eucharist is both sacrifice and meal, since it is offered to the Father and since we consume Christ's body and blood in communion. As a sacrifice, it is the same sacrifice that the incarnate Son offered to the Father, and therefore it brings down upon the Church the divine mercy and strength.

Just as Christ's humanity concealed his divinity, so also we see bread and wine but Christ's body and blood are truly present. Through our sharing in the Eucharist, our souls and bodies are configured to Christ's sacrifice. The Eucharist heals us of sins committed after baptism by drawing us into the mercy of God through our participation in Christ's Cross. So long as we commune in faith, we eat and drink spiritual medicine in the Eucharist, which inebriates us with love and purifies our carnal desires.

---

[10] Ibid., 240.

When at the Last Supper Christ gave his body and blood to his disciples, he did this "so that they would not forget His example."[11] He gave his life out of love for us; we also are to give our lives out of love, imitating his example. Christ's body and blood strengthen us to follow his example. Since Christ unites us to himself in the Eucharist, we do not suffer alone when we suffer for his sake; we suffer in him, and so he suffers in us. This does not mean that he undergoes further suffering, but rather it means that when we are in him eucharistically, we do nothing alone but everything with him. Since we are weak even despite the outpouring of the grace of the Holy Spirit, we need the sacrament of the Eucharist to take away our venial sins and gladden us in the presence of Christ's merciful love, so that we "might faithfully believe in God with joyful and sincere hearts and never cease with devoted ardor to help the wretched."[12] If we fear that Christ's body and blood are not really present in the Eucharist, we should recall that this miracle is certainly within the divine power to accomplish. The manna and animal sacrifices that God gave to Israel foreshadowed the sacrament of the Eucharist, which is the true bread of heaven.

Hildegard also explores why it is fitting that the eucharistic elements be wheaten bread and grape wine; here she focuses on the virginal conception of Jesus Christ, his sinlessness, and his mercy and justice. We should "receive the sweet and pure bread, which is His body, consecrated on the altar by divine invocation, without any bitterness but with sincere affection, and thus escape from humanity's inner hunger and attain to the banquet of eternal beatitude."[13] Similarly, just as we must drink in order to sustain our bodily life, when we receive Christ's blood we are strengthened in the sanctification of new life. The eucharistic wine is mixed with water because blood and water, symbolizing Christ's divinity and humanity, came forth from his wounded side on the Cross. The Eucharist sacramentally represents the mystery of Christ's Paschal sacrifice, and so it is appropriate that the signification of the Eucharist include not only Christ's spilling of his blood but also the water that flowed from his side. Hildegard quotes Proverbs 9.5, "Come, eat my bread, and drink the wine that I have mixed for you."

---

[11] Ibid., 250.
[12] Ibid., 252.
[13] Ibid., p. 255.

Inspired also by the Song of Songs (interpreted mystically), Hildegard says that Christ nourishes the Church with the Eucharist so "that I [Hildegard] may find You in the bread and wine of the divine mystery, the sacrament without deception or artifice. And thus I may kiss You, for You were incarnate for my salvation, and You now make me a sharer in your body and blood."[14] Although Christ has ascended to the right hand of the Father, he can still be found. Hildegard emphasizes the intimacy of our sharing in the incarnate Son. This intimacy is possible because by his "ardent charity" (the Holy Spirit), God the Father transforms the bread and wine on the altar into his Son's body and blood.[15] God has the power to work this miracle in his created things. Again Hildegard comments on the manna, but this time to show that some gain more benefit from the Eucharist than do others. If the Eucharist is like a nuptial kiss between Christ and his bride, then those who receive it with deeper faith will obtain more of its graces. Faith requires believing in things that are not seen, including the mystery that Christ's body and blood are truly present in the Eucharist. The use of bread, wine, and water stimulates our faith because this triad points to the mystery of the divine Trinity. Hildegard urges that we should receive both the body and the blood, rather than refusing the cup. She concludes by describing the various spiritual states in which communicants approach the altar.

The sacrament of holy orders has as its central purpose the celebration of the Eucharist. Hildegard envisions that the priest who is celebrating the sacrament of the Eucharist should "invoke with his words Almighty God, faithfully believing in Him, offering Him in devotion of heart a pure oblation and speaking the words of salvation in the service of humility."[16] The priest who offers the sacrifice must himself be in a state of grace so that he can eat and drink the sacrament; otherwise he should not dare to celebrate the Eucharist. The priest must use the eucharistic prayers and the words of institution that have been handed down in the Church, rather than substituting other words. Since Christ "represented in Himself all ecclesiastical ranks," priests must follow his pattern

---

[14] Ibid., pp. 259–60.
[15] Ibid., p. 260.
[16] Ibid., p. 246.

of life so as to be able to offer his sacrifice at the altar. The priest must be married solely to the Church or to "the justice of God;" otherwise the priest would have to occupy two roles, one secular (husband and father) and one sacred (priest), which would result in the diminishment of the latter vocation.[17] Like Christ, the priest should set an example in foregoing "carnal bonds for the glory of the celestial inheritance."[18] Certainly the Church in earlier eras had married priests, but the Church can now afford to insist that priests devote themselves entirely to the family that is the congregation.

Hildegard also warns that men must be consecrated as priests before they can serve churches. She describes how the apostles, sent by the risen Lord, "collected workers who would strengthen her [the Church] in the Catholic faith and make themselves into priests and bishops and all the ecclesiastical orders."[19] The Church is composed of priests, vowed religious, and laity. Since priests are pastors of the flock whose purpose is to lead the flock to union with the risen Christ through true worship, those who seek the priesthood for personal glory corrupt it utterly. They imitate Satan, "who wanted the highest honor for himself and was cast out of glorious happiness into death."[20] To become a priest or bishop, one must be chosen and anointed properly. Hildegard also considers that women cannot be priests, because the eucharistic signification requires that the priest be male so as to represent Christ in the midst of his bride the Church. Yet this does not displace women from receiving all the benefits of faith: "in her Bridegroom [Christ] she has the priesthood and all the ministry of My altar, and with Him possesses all its riches."[21]

The sacrament of penance has an important role due to the weakness of believers. Baptism, confirmation, and the Eucharist powerfully confer the grace of the Holy Spirit, but our fallen inclination toward sin is not thereby removed. God instructs Hildegard that "if anyone labors under too great a number of these tendencies and is not able to resist them by himself, let him with

---

[17] Ibid., p. 272.
[18] Ibid., p. 275.
[19] Ibid., p. 202.
[20] Ibid., p. 270.
[21] Ibid., p. 278.

devoted purpose seek Me and humbly uncover to Me the wounds of his heart. How? Let him lay bare these wounds to Me by making a humble confession to a priest."[22] Whereas baptism accomplishes a "resurrection" of fallen souls, confession brings about a "second resurrection."[23] By contrast, when confronted with his sin, Adam did not truly confess but instead blamed Eve. When motivated by repentance, the confession of sins (no matter how heinous) to a priest removes the sinner's guilt and restores the sinner to life. After one has confessed one's sins, one receives a penance from the priest. This penance can include prayer, mortification of the flesh, and almsgiving. In these ways the forgiven sinner becomes more deeply configured to Christ. Hildegard especially emphasizes almsgiving, by which we show mercy to others in the name of Christ.

In all times, God has ensured that the human race has had some people who were able to help others in spiritual difficulties. Since the time of the apostles, God has provided us with priests. Priests are the ministers of Christ, and they mediate sacramentally his forgiveness of sins. Christ bestowed upon his priests the power of the keys, the power of binding and loosing the guilt of sin. God commands (in Hildegard's words) that "if a transgressor is penitent, you will loose on earth the chain you fastened on him in his rebellion, and it will be loosed in the secret places of Heaven, for God does not reject the groans of a devout heart."[24] When a priest is not available, people can confess to another person or simply to God directly if death is imminent, although normally Christ wills to work through his ministers, not least because they witness to the penitence of the one who humbly confesses. What about wicked priests? On behalf of God, Hildegard warns them sternly that they will answer for it. Priests do not have the power to forgive sins on their own, but rather this power comes solely from Christ. The reason for this is that "like cannot loose like from a chain; a greater one must come who can save him . . . [N]o person born in sin could deliver sinful humanity from the perdition of death."[25] Only Christ could do this.

---

[22] Ibid., p. 281.
[23] Ibid.
[24] Ibid., p. 287.
[25] Ibid., p. 289.

Hildegard treats marriage in the context of the marriage of Adam and Eve. This context was singled out by Jesus when he gave his approval to marriage. Jesus showed that the marriage of Adam and Eve, which was monogamous and life-long, is the model for Christian marriage, as opposed to the polygamy and divorce allowed in the Old Testament. Hildegard thinks of the begetting and raising of a child as the embodiment of a husband and wife's life-long love for each other. She observes that "a man and woman become one flesh in a union of holy love for the multiplication of the human race. And therefore there should be perfect love in these two," namely the husband and wife.[26] Their "perfect love" is worked out in a lifetime of shared caring for each other and their children. This includes the act of sexual intercourse, in which husband and wife must cooperate and work together, although what is necessary for the love of husband and wife is not sexual intercourse but above all a shared "right faith and pure love of the knowledge of God."[27] Infertile couples are called to be open to children, who come ultimately not from human arrangement but "from the divine disposition and ordination."[28]

Aware that marriage is a friendship, Hildegard requires that husband and wife "shall not tear each other to pieces by viperous rending, but they shall love with pure love, since both man and woman could not exist without having been conceived in such a bond."[29] Neither husband nor wife can violate this love by getting rid of the other, as is the case with divorce. Similarly, people should marry each other only when both of them are mature in age. She urges that "husband and wife cannot be divided from each other but must walk together in one will."[30] An exception arises when one or both of them have committed adultery; in such a case, they can live apart but cannot remarry while their spouse is alive. Hildegard limits licit sexual intercourse to the sole purpose of begetting children and argues that otherwise married couples should live together without sexual intercourse. We need not follow her here, but we must take seriously her warning against allowing lust a foothold in

---

[26] Ibid., pp. 77–8.
[27] Ibid., p. 79.
[28] Ibid.
[29] Ibid., p. 78.
[30] Ibid.

marriage. Certainly all acts of marital intercourse should be open to the possibility of procreation.

The seventh and last sacrament, the anointing of the sick (extreme unction), is generally received when a person will soon die. As a young woman, Teresa of Avila became gravely ill and lost consciousness for four days, during which she was expected to die. She reports in her autobiography that "they gave me the sacrament of the anointing of the sick, and from hour to hour or moment to moment they thought I was going to die; they did nothing but recite the Creed to me, as if I were able to understand them."[31] Her regret was that she had not been allowed to confess her sins when her illness was worsening, before she lost consciousness. In writing about the event, she rejoices that God healed her, and she sees in God's action perhaps even the sparing of her soul from everlasting condemnation. After recovering her health, she nursed her beloved father on his deathbed. His was a joy-filled death. After receiving the anointing of the sick, he counseled those who were attending him and begged them "to recommend him to God and ask mercy for him and always to serve God and reflect on how all things come to an end."[32] He died while reciting the Creed with those around him.

Teresa's two descriptions of the sacrament of the anointing of the sick portray very well the graces that it communicates. On the one hand, the anointing of the sick can assist bodily healing, as it may have done in Teresa's own case. On the other hand, the anointing of the sick more normally prepares people spiritually to meet the difficult task of dying well. The sacrament strengthens people to face the physical and mental suffering that dying imposes, and to do so above all with a deepened awareness of Christ's presence and of the need to prepare one's soul for the encounter with him in the life to come. The sacrament helps us to repent of our sins and to persevere in love for God until the end.

In the spiritual life, the Eucharist has the central place. Teresa speaks of experiencing "such ardent desires to receive Communion that I don't think they could be exaggerated."[33] She finds herself

---

[31] Teresa of Avila, *The Collected Works of St. Teresa of Avila*, Vol. 1, p. 50.
[32] Ibid., p. 62.
[33] Ibid., p. 274.

literally in rapture upon entering a church where Jesus is present in the Eucharist. Thérèse of Lisieux describes her preparations for receiving the Eucharist: "When I am preparing for Holy Communion, I picture my soul as a piece of land and I beg the Blessed Virgin to remove from it *any rubbish* that would prevent it from being *free*; then I ask her to set up a huge tent worthy of *heaven*, adorning it with *her own* jewelry; finally I invite all the angels and saints to come and conduct a magnificent concert there."[34] She wants to be fully prepared for welcoming Christ into her heart, and not only Christ but also his body, the communion of saints. To receive the Eucharist is already to enter into eternal life. Gertrud the Great likewise sees the Eucharist as an anticipation of the heavenly banquet. About to receive communion, she feels that Christ is inviting her to sit with him by God the Father in glory and to "eat at his table with him;" Christ prepares her by giving her "his own jewels."[35] She also understands herself as participating through the Eucharist in "offering the Lord the sacrifice of the Lord's body," thereby spreading the benefits of Christ's Cross.[36] The humility of Christ in the Eucharist amazes and inspires her.

Elizabeth of the Trinity reminds us that the sacrament of penance is a richly positive reality despite its association with sin and punishment; after all, this sacrament fully brings about the forgiveness of our sins by uniting us anew to the power of Christ's Cross. She remarks to her friend Framboise de Sourdon, "how often you have been justified by the sacrament of penance and by all those touches of God in your soul, without you even being aware of it!"[37] Maria Faustina Kowalska has a vision of Jesus forgiving her through the ministry of the priest. She had been ill and unable to go to confession. The priest came to her room, heard her confession, and gave her a penance; and she suddenly saw Jesus—although the vision disappeared immediately. She observes simply that "something was wondrously transpiring in my heart during this confession."[38] The forgiveness of sins itself can be an extraordinary experience. The

---

[34] Thérèse of Lisieux, *Story of a Soul*, p. 172.
[35] Gertrud the Great, *The Herald of God's Loving-Kindness: Book Three*, p. 79.
[36] Ibid.
[37] Elizabeth of the Trinity, *Complete Works*, Vol. 1, trans. Aletheia Kane, O. C. D. (Washington, D.C.: ICS Publications, 1984), p. 127.
[38] Maria Faustina Kowalska, *Diary*, p. 322.

awareness that we have sinned and have truly hurt other people and ourselves produces a deep wound in our conscience. We may think that God could hardly care about us now, let alone love us. Julian of Norwich says about such a person that suddenly "contrition seizes him by the inspiration of the Holy Spirit and turns bitterness into hope of God's mercy."[39] Led by the Holy Spirit, we return to the sacrament of confession, and offer in a spirit of repentance a full accounting of what we have done and receive our penance. Julian explains that "every sinful soul must be healed by these medicines," and she adds that our wounds, when healed, "are not seen by God as wounds but as honours,"[40] because we have overcome through repentance and penance and, in the end, won a victory of love by means of the grace of the Holy Spirit.

Nor should the power of the sacrament of marriage be neglected. The marriage of the parents of Thérèse of Lisieux is justly famous. Her mother died when Thérèse was small, but she remembered her mother well and she drew upon her mother's letters to depict the atmosphere of the family. We can recognize the goodness of what Elisabeth Leseur, herself married to a nonbeliever, writes in a letter to her niece Marie at the time of Marie's first communion: "Later on, when you have your own family, you will make your home a warm and lively center of influence, and you will be a guiding spirit for those who live in the light that you spread. You will be a friend and companion to your husband, and a guide and model of moral strength to your children."[41] Elisabeth says that it will be important for Marie to become educated and to work to improve society, and she observes that "everything done for the family enhances the greatness and strength of peoples and societies."[42] This sounds almost too mundane for the spiritual life, but the intimacy of marriage and the raising of children are central to our lives (not only as adults, but as people who grow up in families) and belong to the sacramental mediation of the grace of the Holy Spirit through the power of Christ's Cross. Jane de Chantal wrote letters to her daughter that offer, from her own experience as a married woman,

---

[39] Julian of Norwich, *Showings*, p. 244.
[40] Ibid., p. 245.
[41] Elisabeth Leseur, *Selected Writings*, ed. and trans. Janet K. Ruffing, R. S. M. (New York: Paulist Press, 2005), p. 175.
[42] Ibid., p. 174.

a profound understanding of the joys and difficulties of married life.[43] Catherine of Siena puts her advice to married couples in a simple form: "All our actions, spiritual or temporal, are directed according to God . . . If we are in the state of marriage, we live in a well-ordered way, treating marriage as a sacrament."[44]

Building on her image of the Church as a wine cellar that contains Christ's blood from which "all the sacraments derive their life-giving power," Catherine holds that the ministerial priesthood, under the stewardship of the successor of Peter, serves to distribute the power of Christ's blood through the sacraments.[45] God explains to Catherine that although we are created to love, it is in baptism that God prepares us to share in love. Only love sustains and nourishes our life, but we must be set aflame in love by God. Sin drenches and puts out the flame of love in us. Without this flame, we cannot benefit from receiving Christ in the Eucharist. Those who have preserved their baptismal purity or have reignited their light "with the fire of true contrition" in the sacrament of penance, will find this light increased by receiving the true light, Jesus Christ, in the Eucharist.[46] She compares the Eucharist to the sun: "just as the sun cannot be divided, so neither can my wholeness as God and as human in this white host."[47] We share in the warmth of this "sun" to differing degrees, depending on the strength of our desire to be united to Christ.

The Eucharist serves as the food and drink of Christian pilgrims. United in faith, we travel not only toward Christ but also in Christ; we anticipate eternal life even as we travel toward it. In addition to the image of a journey, Catherine uses the image of spiritual battle. The refreshment that we find at the "hostel" of the Church enables us to face this journey or battle. God tells Catherine, "My charity sets this blood before you in the hostel of the mystic body of holy Church to give courage to those who would be true knights and fight against their selfish sensuality and weak flesh."[48] The Eucharist even

---

[43] See Francis de Sales, Jane de Chantal, *Letters of Spiritual Direction*, trans. Péronne Marie Thibert, V. H. M. (New York: Paulist Press, 1988), pp. 213–17.

[44] Catherine of Siena, *The Letters of Catherine of Siena*, Vol. 3, trans. Suzanne Noffke, O. P. (Temple, AZ: Arizona Center for Medieval and Renaissance Studies, 2007), p. 34. Catherine advises that married couples observe periodic abstinence.

[45] Catherine of Siena, *The Dialogue*, p. 215.

[46] Ibid., p. 209.

[47] Ibid., p. 207.

"inebriates" those who consume it, so that they do not mind giving their lives for Christ and conquering their vices. There are two ways that Christian pilgrims or knights can communicate in the Eucharist: sacramentally and spiritually. If we communicate only spiritually, this means that for some reason or other we cannot partake of the sacrament even though we desire to do so. If we communicate only sacramentally, we gain no benefit from the Eucharist because our heart is not in our outward action. The best thing is to communicate sacramentally and spiritually at the same time, so that we partake fully in Christ's love that we find in the Eucharist.[49]

Conclusion

Through the sacraments, God applies the saving power of Christ's Cross to heal and elevate our lives, so that even here and now we are drawn into God's own life of Trinitarian love. The sacramental life makes clear that we are on a journey and that Christ Jesus, through the Holy Spirit, is with us every step of the way, uniting us to himself, healing and restoring us, strengthening us for spiritual battle, and guiding us to the Father. This journey is not that of an isolated individual but that of a member of Christ's body the Church. On our journey we depend upon others for the mediation of Christ's power and presence; Christ thereby forms us in receptivity rather than self-sufficiency, and also shows his own glorious humility. The sacraments underscore that Christian life is neither an angelic existence nor a merely intellectual union with God. Rather, the details of birth, food and drink, public activity, and death belong to the sacramental life. So too do the visible ways in which charitable communion manifests itself: marriage and holy orders in the Church. By enabling us to be united to Christ's Cross (and thus to his Resurrection) through the sacraments, God enables us to live the call to holiness. We do so in a constant struggle with sin, whose depth the Cross itself measures. The Christian life consists in an ever-expanding love, which involves all Christians in self-sacrifice, service, and discipline, and which unfolds constantly under the rubric of God's incredible gifts of love and mercy.

---

[48] Ibid., p. 143.
[49] See ibid., p. 123.

6

The Church

How should we think about the Church? In the Rules of the Daughters of Charity, founded by Louise de Marillac and Vincent de Paul, we get a glimpse of the Church's mission in the world. The opening sentence reads, "The principal end for which God has called and established the Daughters of Charity is to honor our Lord Jesus Christ as the source and model of all charity, serving him corporally and spiritually in the person of the poor, whether sick, children, prisoners, or others."[1] To serve others, and especially the poor, imitates Christ who served us out of pure love when we could not help ourselves. The Church, indeed, is the community of Christ's poor, since we are all poor in the sense of being utterly dependent upon Christ Jesus for the charity that, by the grace of the Holy Spirit, unites us to God and to each other.

When we love God and neighbor in Christ, we find ourselves caught up into Christ's self-sacrificial love. Louise de Marillac urges her sisters first and foremost "to keep in mind God and his glory."[2] As a God-centered community, the Church recognizes that everything comes from God's gifting. In Christ, the people of God glorify God. The love of God takes concrete form in worship, which unites the Church in faith and builds the Church in charity. Since this worship is eucharistic, it configures worshippers to the image of Christ who gave himself out of love for us. Louise instructs the Daughters of Charity to imitate Christ by serving the poor "from

---

[1] Vincent de Paul and Louise de Marillac, *Rules, Conferences, and Writings*, ed. Frances Ryan, D. C., and John E. Rybolt, C. M. (New York: Paulist Press, 1995), p. 169.
[2] Ibid., p. 240.

the heart—inquiring of them what they might need; speaking to them gently and compassionately; procuring necessary help for them without being too bothersome or too eager."[3] Material assistance does not constitute the primary goal of the Daughters of Charity, just as it was not Christ's first goal either. Rather, Louise says, "Above all, you must have great care for their salvation, never leaving a poor person or a patient without having uttered some good word. When you meet someone who appears quite ignorant, have them make acts of faith, contrition, and love; for example, 'I believe all that the Holy Church believes, and I wish to live and to die in this faith.'"[4]

Guided by the Holy Spirit, each member plays a role in the Church's mission. Louise asks the Daughters of Charity to be vigilant about getting to bed by 9 p.m., so that they can wake up at 4 a.m. without becoming exhausted by lack of sleep; they will then have time to accomplish all that they need to do. Louise considers that they must be strictly obedient to their Rules or else their mission will go unfulfilled. She warns that "a Sister who does not know how she should act would be in great danger of becoming a source of disedification to persons in the world . . . Little by little, she would become lax, thereby rendering herself unworthy of the graces of God."[5]

Each vocation in the Church, whether clerical, religious, or lay, has certain rules without which the mission of that vocation will not be fulfilled. It would not do, however, first to understand the Church (or any vocation in the Church) in terms of rules. Hildegard of Bingen envisions the Church first as Christ's bride. This biblical image expresses the key reality that the Church exists in a relationship of love with Jesus Christ. As bride, the Church is also mother, because she brings forth many sons and daughters in the Son. God shows to Hildegard "the Bride of My Son, who always bears her children by regeneration in the Spirit and in water, for the strong Warrior founded her on a wide base of virtue, that she might hold and perfect the great crowd of His elect."[6] Baptism and the other sacraments of faith enable the Church to live in charity. Christ gives the Church these sacraments as her foundation, and

---

[3] Ibid., p. 244.
[4] Ibid.
[5] Ibid., p. 251.
[6] Hildegard of Bingen, *Scivias*, p. 170.

they strengthen her in the virtues that unite us to God both now and forever. The sacraments and the virtues build up the body of Christ as "a firm edifice of holy souls," founded by Christ on the apostles and martyrs.[7]

It is Christ who draws people into his Church. At the same time, the Church as bride and mother knows how to draw people and to nourish their faith. The fulfillment of the Church will take place when she rises to eternal life with Christ at the end of time, never to suffer any more. For the time being, she not only endures trials but also continues to give birth to more children of God through baptism. Assisted by the angels, she nourishes their virtues and offers them as a holy sacrifice to God. Because of the greatness of the divine realities that she proclaims, the Church's teaching cannot be understood through reason alone, but requires faith. The Virgin Mary is the model of the Church's purity, truth, and bearing of children for God. Like Mary, the Church bears children by the power of the Holy Spirit and without any corruption of her integrity and unity of faith, despite the trials that she endures.

The main task of the Church is "to worship the One God in the true Trinity."[8] To do this, the Church's members must have true faith rather than an idolatrous conception of God. They must also have their sins washed away. So as to make this true worship possible for the baptized, the Holy Spirit illumines the Church so that she knows and follows the divine law, even though some of the baptized rebel against this law (as Adam did). The grace of baptism enables the children of the Church to follow God's law and to resist temptation and falsehood. In Noah and Abraham, the coming of Christ and Church formed by baptism were prefigured. God tells Hildegard, "The circumcision of baptism sprang from the baptism of My Son, and so it shall remain till the last day, and then its sanctity will abide for eternity and know no end."[9] Faith and baptism, which unite us with Christ, are at the center of the Church. Christ's Holy Spirit vivifies us in baptism and gives us faith.

The faith of the Church comes from Christ, who communicated it to the apostles. Thus the Church's apostolic teaching and structure are never optional. The apostles tasked the bishops and priests

---

[7] Ibid.
[8] Ibid., p. 174.
[9] Ibid., p. 181.

who succeeded them with "carrying the health-giving chrisms and announcing the divine law to the people" of all nations.[10] Together, the Church's "three institutions"—clergy, religious, and laity— "surround and consolidate the blessed Church in a wondrous way in honor of the heavenly Trinity."[11] Hildegard states that "when the innocent Lamb was lifted up on the altar of the cross for human salvation, the Church suddenly appeared in Heaven by a profound mystery, in purity of faith and all the other virtues; and by the Supreme Majesty she was joined to the Only-Begotten of God."[12] Everything that the Church has comes from Christ's sacrificial gift of his body and blood for the salvation of the world in fulfillment of God's covenants and promises with his people Israel.

Catherine of Siena emphasizes the image of the Church as a vineyard (cf. John 15). The Father is the gardener; the Son is the vine. We are the branches of the vine. As a vineyard, the Church needs ministers to weed and nourish the vineyard. The role of priests in the vineyard that is the Church consists in "administering the blood to you through the sacraments you receive from them, and. . .planting grace within you."[13] Although Catherine lived during a time when the bishop of Rome was resident in Avignon and when the bishops were fomenting schism, Catherine not only does not abandon her understanding of the Church as God's holy vineyard, but rather presses it even more. Writing to the Italian Pope Urban VI three days before the election of an antipope, Catherine tells Urban that "you have been made his [Christ's] vicarerU and cellarer; you have the keys of the blood, the blood in which we were created anew to grace."[14] The image is that of a vineyard's wine steward, who has the keys to the cellar and governs the distribution of the wine. Catherine calls upon Urban to use his authority to discipline the Church's priests so that selfish love does not continue to flourish in them.

Catherine admits that when she looks at the Church that Urban governs, she sees "the hell of sin upon sin, with the poison of selfish love."[15] This sad sight could lead her in one of two directions;

[10] Ibid., p. 203.
[11] Ibid., p. 216.
[12] Ibid., p. 238.
[13] Catherine of Siena, *The Dialogue*, p. 60.
[14] Catherine of Siena, *The Letters of Catherine of Siena*, p. 213.
[15] Ibid., p. 216.

either she could consider the evil to be the fruit of an inherently bad institution, or she could argue for the goodness of the apostolic structure and call for its reform through personal conversion and pastoral discipline. She chooses to affirm the goodness of the Church's apostolic structure, and the goodness of God's permission of the election of Urban as bishop of Rome, despite what might seem to be strong evidence against it. Indeed, she says that in Siena the bishop has allowed his church to become "such a wretched robbers' den that it's a wonder the earth isn't swallowing us up."[16]

Writing to three Italian bishops who were at first loyal to Urban but had wavered, Catherine warns them that they have failed the Church by undermining the Church's apostolic unity. They need to "leave death behind and return to life by standing united in faith and obedience to Pope Urban VI."[17] She blames them for failing to love God's truth in a steadfast manner. They have instead been "shifting about like a leaf in the wind."[18] They have not protected the bride of Christ, the Church, at a time when she was threatened by schism. Instead they have allowed the bride of Christ to be riven in schism without even raising their voices against this. Pope Urban has the authority granted by God through a regular papal election; the antipope Clement's authority comes solely from a group of bishops usurping to themselves the power to rebel against a duly elected Pope and to elect their own Pope. They are condemned from their own mouths because they themselves earlier proclaimed the truth that Urban had been duly elected Pope. She reminds them that they had asked and received papal favors from Urban, and she reminds them of the solemn rites of his ascension to the papacy and of the reverence they had freely paid him. In choosing falsehood over the very truth that they proclaimed by their mouths and to which they bore witness by their actions, they have allied themselves with the devil and the antichrist.

Catherine underscores that like wolves among sheep, these bishops have chosen a luxurious personal life over the reform of the Church and the salvation of souls. Personal sin, however, does not destroy the truth or grace of the office of bishop. She writes,

---

[16] Ibid.
[17] Ibid., p. 219.
[18] Ibid., p. 220.

"I long with tremendous desire to see you rising up from darkness and uniting yourself with light."[19] She begs them to return to true service to Christ's Church. In a later letter to Queen Giovanna d'Angiò of Naples, Catherine repeats her view that the problem is not "the mystic body of holy Church" (by which she means the apostolically governed visible Church) but rather is the misdeeds of bishops who elected another "pope" for reasons unrelated to the Church's mission. Catherine knows that "though contrary winds may for a while set the little ship of holy Church adrift, still neither she nor those who trust her will perish."[20]

Catherine's understanding of the Church certainly does not suppose that the Church is composed of sinless beings. Although the sins of believers wound the Church terribly, the Church's holiness does not depend on the holiness of believers. The success of those who profess to follow Christ requires a strenuous purification of their loves. In times of persecution, we can hope that believers will stand up to the trial by God's grace, but we cannot assume that this will be the case. Catherine did not change her view of the Church because of the sins of so many priests and lay people; she already knew how weak humans were. The faults of our neighbors will not shock us if we know our own faults and if we recall Christ's endurance of the Cross. Catherine compares the present discord to the conflicts between Christ and his disciples. It thus makes sense to Catherine that Church follows a painful path: "For by drowning our selfish sensual will in suffering and hard work, we draw nearer to our Creator and become one will with him. So we have to suffer; we have to lose ourselves, and then we will be able to weep and offer continual humble prayer in God's presence for his honor and the salvation of souls."[21]

Even so, should not Christ have known better than to hand himself over to his sinful disciples and their apostolic successors the bishops? Catherine reminds us that Christ himself deliberately handed himself over into the hands of sinners for our salvation. These sinners included his disciples who betrayed him and fled from him in his hour of need. Because we are sinners, even the Church

---

[19] Ibid., p. 224.
[20] Ibid., p. 289.
[21] Ibid., pp. 131–2.

will not be a refuge from sin, although the Church is interiorly holy through the grace of Christ's Holy Spirit. Catherine urges her friend Monna Alessa dei Saracini "to renew your weeping and desire with many prayers for the salvation for the whole world and for the reform of holy Church."[22] The Church's holiness in truth and in the sacraments is not opposed to the fact that the Church also needs reform. Rather, the reform that configures us to Christ is what we all need, and to undertake this reform requires the discipline of suffering. Catherine urges that "if we servants ransomed by that blood want to be faithful spouses, let's not sleep. No, let's rouse ourselves from the slumber of apathy and run along this way of Christ crucified with yearning and breathless desire."[23]

Having diagnosed our problem as "selfish sensual will," she recognizes that Christ comes to us always as a gift; the apostolic structure of the Church teaches us receptivity, since we must receive Christ from the hands of (sinful) others. Learning to receive Christ from the hands of sinners like ourselves enables us to apprehend his humility and to imitate it. Catherine never countenances the abuses, but her position is not one of despair in the face of sin. Speaking of the "stormy sea" of mortal life, she observes that "because we would never be able to cross this stormy sea without suffering, this gentle loving Word, who endured suffering, made himself our way and our rule, cementing the road with his own blood."[24] She has confidence that God will hear the prayers of believers for holy Church. But since we are sinners, the Church, like the world, will always be in need of discipline and renewal in holiness.

Catherine never doubts that the Church faithfully communicates to believers the salvific wine of Christ's blood and the nourishment of his truth. She depicts "holy Church" as a mother who nurtures her children at her breasts with the life-giving milk of truth and the sacraments. God ensures that this life-giving milk cannot be perverted by the sins of particular Christians who harm mother Church. Another image that Catherine uses is that of light. God is on the side of the light, and the only thing that the schismatics can do is to create a bit of temporary fog. Catherine urges Queen

---

[22] Ibid., p. 132.
[23] Ibid.
[24] Ibid.

Giovanna to receive gratefully "the good life and teaching that Christ's vicar wants to give to those who are nourished at the breast of his bride."[25] The nourishment that we receive from mother Church consists in the charity that flows to us sacramentally from Christ's Cross through the grace of the Holy Spirit. At the heart of Catherine's vision is the fiery love of God the Trinity who pours himself out for the redemption of sinners.

Gertrud the Great can also help us. In prayer, she receives a vision of the Church. She records that "the King of glory, the Lord Jesus Christ, appeared to her [Gertrud] . . . in the form of his own body, the mystical body of the Church, whose bridegroom and head he condescends to be called and to be."[26] What does she notice about this "body"? On the right side, she sees nothing but glory. Here the body, that is, the Church, is "solemnly distinguished with royal garments."[27] But the left side of the body is entirely the opposite. The left side shows Jesus as "naked and entirely full of sores."[28] What is the meaning of this? The Church is perfect in her head, Jesus. As his body, however, the Church is not yet fully perfected. By the grace of the Holy Spirit, some believers have come to enjoy already the glory that the head possesses. These believers constitute, as it were, the "right side" of Jesus' body the Church. Here the Church's "royal garments" have as ornaments the saints and those who love to lift up the righteous. But other believers have not yet arrived at perfect holiness, and indeed can be quite imperfect. They are still "full of sores."

What should the Church do about those who profess faith in Christ and yet shame Christ by being "full of sores"? Gertrud notes that some people would apply severe discipline against the imperfect. In her view this would be a mistake. The problem is that by attacking others, we can fall into the very lack of charity that we are condemning. As she puts it with respect to those who would apply severe discipline, "These people seem to batter the Lord's sores furiously with their fists, and from those sores corrupted matter, expelled by the sudden assault, seems to fly out in their faces

---

[25] Ibid., p. 291.
[26] Gertrud the Great, *The Herald of God's Loving-Kindness: Book* 3, p. 210.
[27] Ibid.
[28] Ibid.

(that is, of the critics), infecting them and contaminating them."[29] Rather than being contaminated with lack of charity, the way to respond to the sins of members of the Church is to focus even more strongly upon the charity of the saints. Gertrud suggests that this path constitutes the reliable source of renewal for the Church in every age, because charity is inflamed primarily by the witness of the saints.

In Gertrud's vision, Jesus simply "pretends to ignore" the sinners and the sores that they inflict upon his body.[30] Instead he focuses his gaze on those who love him and on those who love his saints. The Church's holiness is found in Jesus and his holy people, and when we look at the Church we should concentrate our attention not on the sinners but on the saints. Only in this way will we discover the Church's holiness and have our hearts inflamed with love rather than being pulled down by focusing on the sins of believers. Jesus, the merciful one, looks on his Church in his perfect charity, and he sees love despite the "sores." By the grace of the Holy Spirit, the merits of those who love bring about the conversion and healing of the Church, as Jesus applies his mercy to sinners. Gertrud says that "the kindly Lord, overcome by his own loving-kindness and stimulated by the love of his special friends . . . gazes on the ornaments of the benefits lavished on his special friends and wipes away those stains with his right-hand garment, that is, for the sake of the merits of his chosen."[31]

Jesus also instructs Gertrud in the best way to handle our fellow believers' sins. If we see that our neighbors' failings are wounding the body of Christ, we should first seek to correct these failings "by handling them gently—that is, by gentle reproaches made in love."[32] If this does not work, we can proceed to more stringent reproaches. We cannot refuse to concern ourselves with our neighbors' failings insofar as they wound the Church. This would be to allow the wounds on Christ's body to fester. Jesus tells Gertrud that such "people seem to apply to my wounds a dressing that does not heal but rather makes my wound go rotten and crawl as it were with worms while by their silence they enable their neighbors' failings to

---

[29] Ibid., p. 211.
[30] Ibid.
[31] Ibid.
[32] Ibid.

increase, although they could perhaps have corrected them with a few words."[33] In short, we should care about healing the sores on Christ's body, but our gaze must be focused on Jesus and his love as found in his saints and in those who love them. Otherwise we risk becoming as merciless as those whom we criticize, so that we add to the sores on the left side of Jesus' body rather than taking them away as we hoped to do. We need to join ourselves to the mercy of Jesus who stands "before the Father, pleading for the Church."[34] We can trust that Jesus, who loves us, will take care of his Church by converting sinners not least through the powerful witness of those who love him and who are filled with the grace of the Holy Spirit.

Teresa Benedicta of the Cross (Edith Stein) likewise emphasizes that the Church is the body of Christ. As she says, "Every individual human being is created to be a member of this body."[35] No human is sufficient unto himself or herself, even on a natural level. The temporal "unfolding" of the body of Christ requires ideally the participation of every human being, although not all do in fact cooperate with the grace of the Holy Spirit. When the body of Christ has been brought to fulfillment at the end of time, the Trinity will fully dwell in the human race: "A humanity united in Christ and through Christ is the temple in which the Triune God has his abode."[36] Teresa Benedicta adds that not only humans, but also the angels belong to the Church as Christ's body, because Christ is the head of all rational creatures. Indeed, the whole creation belongs in a certain sense to the Church as the mystical body. Teresa Benedicta explains that God created everything through the Word, and the Word became incarnate in "the total context of the created universe."[37] The Fall in some way affected the whole creation, and all creation awaited the redemptive coming of the Son of God. Although the new creation will renew all things, nonetheless the body of Christ is particularly composed of humans, because "humankind is the portal through which the Word of God entered into the created world."[38] Since the Son became incarnate as a man, Christ is the head of the Church, and the head

---

[33] Ibid.
[34] Ibid., p. 225.
[35] Edith Stein, *Finite and Eternal Being*, p. 526.
[36] Ibid., p. 527.
[37] Ibid.
[38] Ibid.

of all creation, precisely in his human nature which we share with him.

The Church's mission is to spread God's fiery love. As Hadewijch says, "It is to this that Holy Church invites all who are docile to her. May God now come to our assistance!"[39]

Conclusion

The Church is the place where God meets us, by uniting us in charity with Jesus Christ through the Holy Spirit. Through baptism and the Eucharist, Christ builds his Church in love, sanctifying humans who join the angelic choirs in praise of the Father, Son, and Holy Spirit. Love is the purpose of the Church. The Church is God's vineyard, Christ's bride, and our mother. These images express the communication of the divine love that enlivens and sanctifies us, and that fulfills the purpose of the whole creation. With bold humility, Christ gives himself to us through the hands of our fellow sinners. By teaching us to receive from others, he weans us from our pride and guides us to real fellowship with others. We cannot ignore the way in which our sins weaken the Church, but God will not abandon the Church through which he nourishes humankind with saving truth and with life-giving sacraments. In giving thanks for Christ and his gifts, let us give thanks, too, for Christ's body and bride.

---

[39] Hadewijch, *The Complete Works*, trans. Columba Hart, O. S. B. (New York: Paulist Press, 1980), p. 191.

7

The virtues

The Christian life of virtue begins with God's gift of faith. Faith establishes a relationship with God in which we know him as he has revealed himself to be. To describe faith, Catherine of Siena frequently uses the image of enlightenment. The grace of the Holy Spirit enlightens our reason so that we can know the invisible God. The gift of faith enables us to know the invisible God not impersonally, but in and through Jesus Christ. Forgiven and renewed by the power of the Cross, we rejoice in the God who loves us. As God explains to Catherine, "This blood [Christ's] gives you knowledge of the truth when knowledge of yourself leads you to shed the cloud of selfish love. There is no other way to know the truth. In so knowing me the soul catches fire with unspeakable love, which in turn brings continual pain."[1]

Why does charity cause pain? Catherine recognizes that when we come to know sin for what it is, we sorrow because the all-good God is not loved. Charity puts us at odds with worldliness, both in ourselves and as we experience it in others. Charity also leads us to give our lives in service to God and neighbor. "All virtues," God tells Catherine, "are built on charity for your neighbors."[2] We can only love our neighbor when we love God, because it is the love of God that heals us of selfishness. In this regard God instructs Catherine, "Those who do not love me cannot believe or trust me; rather they believe and trust in their selfish sensuality, which they do love."[3] We fail when we try to rely on our own resources; instead we need God to restore us and make us what we should be. The grace of the Holy

---

[1] Catherine of Siena, *The Dialogue*, p. 30.
[2] Ibid., p. 36.
[3] Ibid., p. 38–9.

Spirit configures us to Jesus Christ so that we become willing to die for others out of love, in service to their spiritual and bodily needs. Catherine affirms that the virtues are possessed as a unity. One cannot have love if one lacks justice, for example; nor can one be a just person if one lacks prudence. Yet different persons excel in different virtues. For each person, some virtues come more easily than do others. In loving a particular virtue, however, we love them all because "they are all bound together in loving charity."[4] Why is it, then, that we have certain virtues that are our particular strengths? In answer, God tells Catherine that "I wanted to make you dependent on one another so that each of you would be my minister, dispensing the graces and gifts you have received from me."[5] We must learn how to receive from each other rather than seeking to dominate and use each other. We have to become a community of receivers and givers, modeled on the Trinitarian communion of giving and receiving the divine life.

We know that we have virtues when they are tested, as when insults reveal our patience or lack thereof. Only then can we see whether our virtue is real. When people act in unjust ways to us, we must respond justly rather than trying to take vengeance. Such trials either strengthen our possession of virtue or show that we lack true virtue. God explains to Catherine that, for example, "your kindness and mildness are revealed through gentle patience in the presence of wrath."[6] But do we not often fail when our virtues are tested? Catherine knows that it is so. For this reason, she emphasizes that the interior virtues are more important than external acts and bodily asceticism. When we do good actions out of love, our focus is not on ourselves but on God and neighbor. By contrast, if selfishness remains in control, trials will reveal the emptiness of our supposed virtue.

Catherine recognizes that many times we will be exposed for having retained our selfish love. Rather than excusing this or covering it up, she urges that we make repentance and conversion central to our lives. God instructs Catherine that we should begin by giving praise for the many gifts that God has given us and by confessing

---

[4] Ibid., p. 38.
[5] Ibid.
[6] Ibid., p. 39.

that we have too often shown "ingratitude in the face of so many favors."[7] Once we admit to ourselves the condition in which we really are, we can sincerely regret what we have done. In this way we exercise "the virtue of discernment, rooted in self-knowledge and true humility."[8] Discernment frees us from remaining stuck in our sins, because we love God enough to confront our failings and humble ourselves before him.

Discernment is not of course solely a matter of willingness to acknowledge our sins. Rather, we can equally discern that we have done well; and in so discerning, we see the power of God in our lives because we recognize our own weakness. Catherine describes discernment as being rooted in humble self-knowledge, and humble self-knowledge as being rooted in knowing God. True love of self and love of God are not possible without knowledge of God and knowledge of self (a knowledge destroyed by pride). The circle of virtue requires knowledge and love, not solely love.

Charity, discernment, and humility are like a tree that blossoms fragrantly and bears fruit, namely the fruit that is all the other virtues. God says to Catherine, "What I want is many works of patient and courageous endurance and of the other virtues I have described to you—interior virtues that are all active in bearing the fruit of grace."[9] Interior union with God through charity must be our goal, and external works must serve this goal rather than becoming an end in themselves.

The virtue of discernment does not allow us to judge our neighbor. God instructs Catherine that charitable persons "assume no right to be concerned with the intentions of other people but only with discerning my merciful will."[10] Even if we do see another sin, we must not judge the person's intentions, but instead we should imitate God's compassion and assume that God will draw good out of the evil. Instead of becoming bitter when we see even rampant vice around us, we must take joy in everything, because we know that by different paths (including through many trials), God is bringing his people to salvation. If we are truly in love with God, we will be in love with his will and not be scandalized by

---

[7] Ibid., p. 41.
[8] Ibid.
[9] Ibid., p. 42.
[10] Ibid., p. 190.

what he permits—even though we will not cease to pray and work for the conversion of sinners, ourselves included. Charity should continually increase in the person who loves God: "Those who are not growing are by that very fact going backward."[11] To grow in charity means to continue to beg God for his merciful grace, both for ourselves and for others.

Hildegard of Bingen directs our attention to the seven gifts of the Holy Spirit: wisdom, understanding, counsel, fortitude, knowledge, piety, and fear of the Lord (cf. Isaiah 11.1-2). These gifts, she says, are like pillars that protect the Bride, the Church. By these gifts, we are able to avoid focusing on earthly pleasures and instead to lift up our minds to God. Strengthened by the gifts of the Holy Spirit, we can love God and neighbor by exercising the virtues of justice, fortitude, and sanctity. For Hildegard the key to exercising these virtues is to keep eternity in view rather than seeking earthly gain above all. Only in this way can we fight the spiritual battle that is required by life in Christ, the battle against temptation to sin. To build up justice we must be united to Christ, since it is by Christ's Incarnation that humans were restored to justice. God's wisdom and justice, revealed in Christ, provide the model for human wisdom and justice. Divine justice "bent down from Heaven in the Incarnation of the Savior."[12] Like wisdom, justice is eternal, and we must be conformed to its standard. This is possible for us through Christ. Hildegard states that justice "dwells in the purity of the minds of the just, who direct all their desire toward obeying the justice of God."[13] The just are configured to Christ, who is justice (as is the Father).

Hildegard argues that justice, because it is eternal and divine, lifts us up toward God when we possess it. Injustice, by contrast, causes us to be more attached to what is earthly and passing away. She does not mean that earthly deeds themselves are to be despised for being earthly. On the contrary, just earthly deeds lead us to eternal life. "Earthly" in the negative sense pertains only to unjust earthly deeds, which weigh us down by separating us from divine justice. Fortitude serves justice, in a manner analogous to how a

---

[11] Ibid., p. 186.
[12] Hildegard of Bingen, *Scivias*, p. 467.
[13] Ibid.

prince serves his king. It is by fortitude that we repel all threats to justice. The true enemies of the human person are vices, and we must struggle courageously against them in order to have any hope of remaining in Christ's justice. Merely human bravery would not suffice, Hildegard suggests, for preserving justice. Instead we need God's help. The virtue of fortitude, when given to us by God, "is armed by the power of Almighty God, and, strong in faith, repels the advances of the Devil."[14] Here Hildegard draws from St. Paul's image of putting on spiritual armor so as to sustain life in Christ. The "helmet" of this armor is God's power to save; the "breastplate" is the law of Christ; the "sword" is the Scriptures whose meaning is Christ Jesus. Armed in this way, believers walk bravely in paths of righteousness set forth by the holy teaching of the Church, and believers undertake in Christ "strong and noble works" of love.[15]

For Hildegard, the main threat to virtue is the temptation to pursue earthly pleasures above God. We can only resist such temptation "by thinking of the eternal."[16] Otherwise, we will seize the earthly pleasure no matter what the consequences, with no regard for justice. When we cleave to earthly pleasures over God, we make earthly things our god. Lust, then, is connected with idolatry. It follows that chastity is no small virtue, but instead is a virtue of "mighty daring."[17] Faith and charity conquer lust and idolatry, and this victory is revealed by chastity and true worship. Hildegard praises God for displaying "the vast strength of His pervasive Word to slay all unfaithful idol-worship and other schisms of unbelief."[18]

She also treats sanctity in this context. Sanctity is oriented to the worship of God. The holy person will worship God in all circumstances, "in prosperity and adversity, in human joy and sorrow."[19] The holy person in times of trouble does not become bitter toward God, because the holy person recognizes God as a supremely just judge who will put all things to rights. Hildegard observes that sanctity "is so honorable and sweet and full of heavenly grace that the depth of her mystery exceeds the human

---

[14] Ibid.
[15] Ibid., p. 468.
[16] Ibid.
[17] Ibid.
[18] Ibid.
[19] Ibid.

intellect."[20] We cannot judge our own sanctity or that of others, and yet sanctity does have an outward mark, namely the care that we take to defend our spiritual purity against vices and indeed against those who tempt us to deviate from God's law. The holy person is zealous for the things of God, just as Jesus was in cleansing the Temple. We cannot give ourselves sanctity, but rather it comes to us "through the death of Christ and the pure regeneration of the Spirit and water," since in baptism we share in Christ's death and are freed from our sins.[21]

The great sign of sanctity is Jesus' Cross. Had he been sinful, he could not have suffered with supreme justice and love for the forgiveness of our sins. The Virgin Mary, too, is a model of sanctity, since she was prepared by God for her mission as mother of Christ. When we desire to learn sanctity, we should turn first to Jesus' Cross and then to the entirety of the Scriptures, which are inspired by the Holy Spirit. How much we have attended to the Scriptures (and have received the Holy Spirit who inspired the Scriptures) is shown by whether or not we perform holy works as Jesus did. Interiorly, sanctity should fill us with joy and prevent us from feeling shame at our thoughts and deeds. Hildegard urges that we should live according to goodness and self-sacrifice. Although we tend to think of self-sacrifice in terms of great and notable actions, she points out that it usually takes the form of seeking higher goods over the earthly pleasures that can be acquired by money, power, lust, and so forth. Sanctity cannot be sustained without justice and fortitude.

Just as Hildegard emphasizes that sanctity requires accepting God's will in both prosperity and adversity, Jane de Chantal urges that love for God's will should bring us to "refuse nothing [we] recognize to be His will."[22] We should abandon ourselves entirely to God's providence, and rest assured even in the midst of trials that God is leading us on a wise path to our goal of union with him. Abandonment to God's providence is not merely passive: when we abandon ourselves to God's providential guidance, he will open us more and more to love God and neighbor. He will give us wonderful opportunities for "acts of charity and humility," which "will feed the fire of sacred love which you feel in your heart and

---

[20] Ibid.
[21] Ibid., p. 169.
[22] Jane de Chantal, *Letters of Spiritual Direction*, p. 204.

continually desire."[23] Jane recognizes, however, that this love for and abandonment to God's will does not come easily to us.

In testing our charity, we can ask the following question: do we love God for his own sake, or does what seems to be a love for God actually amount to love for his creatures, so that we in fact prefer created goods? Our desire cannot be satisfied by finite goods; we move on insatiably from one to another. Even if we gained the creature everlastingly but lost God, we could not be happy. When God permits that we lose the temporal things that we most love, we should not become bitter toward God. Rather, we should admit our tendency to cleave to the things of this world, and strive instead to cleave to God and to love all things in him. Jane knows that "our first reactions are inevitable, and our gentle Savior is not offended by them."[24] She simply urges us to be strengthened by the recollection that our lives in this world are intended to prepare us for the world to come.

We can become attached not merely to persons but also to worldly possessions and honors. It can be a very difficult thing to lose a significant amount of money or status. As Jane counsels her daughter prior to her daughter's marriage, "You will be living in plenty, but, my darling, remember always that we are meant to use the good things God gives us without being attached to them. Such is the attitude we should have toward all that the world values."[25] In making her Lenten resolutions, Elisabeth Leseur emphasizes that this effort to detach oneself from love of money or of status must not turn into an external hardness or bitterness. One must maintain "light-heartedness, kindness, friendliness, joy."[26] Elisabeth also seeks to undertake regular almsgiving, "through the gift of my money, my time, my heart, first for those closest to me, then for the neighbor who is further away—especially for the poor, the humble, the suffering."[27]

Elisabeth observes that we can even become attached to the privileges that we receive through faith in Jesus Christ. We can assume an attitude of superiority to our neighbors who do not

[23] Ibid.
[24] Ibid., p. 207.
[25] Ibid., p. 210.
[26] Elisabeth Leseur, *Selected Writings*, p. 115.
[27] Ibid.

share our faith. Just as Christians are often persecuted, so Christians themselves can fall into the trap of persecuting others. This happens, as she says, when "[w]e complacently scorn those who hold different beliefs and think ourselves scarcely obliged to extend our charity to them."[28] At the same time, a central part of her love for nonbelievers, including her own husband, is her continual prayer that God will convert them and unite them with himself.[29]

Regarding the life of Christian virtue, Mother Teresa of Calcutta insists that "love, to be true, has to hurt. I must be willing to give whatever it takes not to harm other people and, in fact, to do good to them. This requires that I be willing to give until it hurts."[30] She associates Jesus in particular with the poor and oppressed. By becoming incarnate and dying on a cross, Jesus identifies with "the hungry one, the naked one, the homeless one, the unwanted one."[31] Jesus tells us that in feeding, welcoming, clothing, or visiting a poor or suffering person, we feed, welcome, clothe, and visit Jesus (see Mt. 25.40). Mother Teresa applies this teaching to a variety of contemporary situations. Seeking to awaken consciences, she asks: "Maybe in our own family we have somebody who is feeling lonely, who is feeling sick, who is feeling worried. Are we there? . . . Are we willing to give until it hurts in order to be with our families, or do we put our own interests first?"[32] These sacrifices are what people look for in order to know that we truly love them.

Mother Teresa applies this understanding of charity also to the abortion of infants in the womb. Given that the United States and many other societies abort millions of infants each year, she observes that "the greatest destroyer of peace today is abortion."[33] Once we accept the killing of infants in the womb, it becomes hardly possible to condemn the other forms of killing that destroy peace around the world. If one accepts the killing of one's own offspring, on what grounds does one repudiate killings in which the perpetrators have far less connection with the ones whom they

---

[28] Ibid., p. 136.
[29] See ibid., p. 125.
[30] Mother Teresa of Calcutta, "Speech of Mother Teresa of Calcutta to the National Prayer Breakfast, Washington, D.C., February 3, 1994," online at www.priestsfor-life.org/brochures/mtspeech, accessed May 2, 2011.
[31] Ibid.
[32] Ibid.
[33] Ibid.

kill? Abortion signals that a society has become willing to pursue its own ends at the cost even of the bond between parent and child. Mother Teresa remarks, "By abortion, the mother does not learn to love, but kills even her own child to solve her problems. . . .Any country that accepts abortion is not teaching its people to love, but to use any violence to get what they want."[34] She adds that people who are very concerned about India's starving or neglected children or about inner-city violence often brush aside concerns about the large-scale killing of innocent infants in the womb. But God loves each infant, and indeed the "unborn child has been carved in the hand of God from conception and is called by God to love and to be loved, not only now in this life, but forever."[35] Since God loves each human being, we must care for each other.

Just as Catherine of Siena urges married couples to love each other reverently rather than with "uncontrolled desire,"[36] Mother Teresa understands that sexual intercourse must express the fullness of the gift of self to one's spouse. Certainly no such gift is possible if the couple has not permanently committed themselves to each other in marriage. One owes it to one's spouse that acts of marital intercourse build up marriage in reverent love. The fullness of the gift of self in marital intercourse requires that the act not purposefully exclude the possibility of begetting of a child. Mother Teresa describes it this way: "In destroying the power of giving life, through contraception, a husband or wife is doing something to self. This turns the attention to self and so it destroys the gift of love in him or her. In loving, the husband and wife must turn the attention to each other as happens in natural family planning, and not to self, as happens in contraception."[37] As she adds, "Once that living love is destroyed by contraception, abortion follows very easily."[38] Mother Teresa encourages us to look for the spiritual riches that a married couple can obtain by ensuring that their marital intercourse embodies the full gift of self. She comments, "We cannot solve all the

---

[34] Ibid.
[35] Ibid.
[36] Catherine of Siena, *The Letters of Catherine of Siena*, Vol. 3, p. 172.
[37] Mother Teresa of Calcutta, "Speech of Mother Teresa of Calcutta."
[38] Ibid.

problems in the world, but let us never bring in the worst problem of all, and that is to destroy love."[39]

We should expect that love will challenge us—as Mother Teresa says, it will "hurt." To follow this path of love, we require the virtues that inform our will and our passions so that we can be courageous when faced with danger, temperate when placed before desirable goods, just when considering what is due to others and to ourselves, and prudent when required to deliberate upon a course of action. The path of love also requires us to renounce things that we could have had, and instead to serve our needy neighbor. Catherine tells her friend Ristoro Canigiani that "acts of compassion and ministering to the poor out of whatever power God has given you is very pleasing to God and redounds to your own salvation."[40] She urges her friend to sell "your superfluous goods and ostentatious clothes," possessions that she even describes as "very detrimental" because such things can only "serve to make the heart vain and to nurture pride by making us think we are better and greater than others, glorying in what we should not glory."[41] She also warns her friend against devoting himself to banqueting rather than to love of God and neighbor.

Writing to the rulers of Florence, Catherine commends courage and justice. What bonds together cities and communities is ultimately charity. Without charity, people will turn against each other rather than holding together in times of trial or when their self-interest no longer requires it. Only charity defeats the "selfish sensuality" that pulls people apart and leads to violence.[42] She tells the rulers of Florence that she longs to see them joined together by charity. In this way they will be filled with courage also, a courage to "fight the world" rather than to give in to worldly selfishness.[43] People who have charity can act bravely on behalf of their neighbors because they do not fear to lose worldly things.

Similarly, charitable people do justice vis-à-vis their neighbors. This is especially important, obviously, for rulers. Catherine says that if charitable people "come into positions of leadership, the

---

[39] Ibid.
[40] Catherine of Siena, *The Letters of Catherine of Siena*, Vol. 3, p. 172.
[41] Ibid.
[42] Ibid., p. 177.
[43] Ibid.

pearl of holy justice is resplendent in them because they hear and do justice to the small as well as to the great, to the poor as well as to the rich. Neither human respect nor bribery nor love for personal profit will make them spoil this virtue of justice."[44] Lacking charity, rulers will be moved by self-interest rather than by justice. Only when rulers possess charity will they have the strength to act for the common good rather than in favor of their own interests and on behalf of their own petty quarrels. Catherine describes justice as "the gentle virtue that reconciles us creatures with our Creator and one citizen with another, because it flows from the fountain of charity."[45] For its part, lack of courage often comes from desiring to please others rather than to take a difficult but necessary step.

Can the use of lethal force in battle or in police action ever be just? Birgitta of Sweden recognizes that, sadly, some soldiers "go to war with deliberate wrath and envy and in a spirit of vengeance."[46] To die in such a condition means to undergo everlasting punishment. How could God permit such a thing to happen? God answers Birgitta that he permits men to go to war in a spirit of vengeful wrath because, in their wrath, they have freely abandoned God and instead have chosen to serve Satan. Yet not all soldiers go to war with the goal of harming others. Rather, their goal may be to protect the innocent persons of the society that they have sworn to protect. Indeed, Birgitta's son Charles was himself a knight. In a vision after Charles's death, Birgitta sees God forgiving him his many sins. One of the grounds upon which God forgives Charles is that he desired "to risk his life willingly in warfare" for a just cause.[47] In certain circumstances, the risking of one's own life in battle can be part of a laudable intention to protect and serve others out of love.

In the Christian life of virtue, obedience also has a special place. God tells Catherine that "eternal life, which had been locked by Adam's disobedience, was unlocked by the key of obedience."[48] Christ's obedient love reversed Adam and Eve's rebellious pride. Obedience, then, "is conceived and born of charity."[49] Fostered by

---

[44] Ibid., p. 178.
[45] Ibid.
[46] Birgitta of Sweden, *Life and Selected Revelations*, p. 108.
[47] Ibid., p. 187.
[48] Catherine of Siena, *The Dialogue*, p. 328.
[49] Ibid., p. 332.

humility, obedience shows itself through patience. Obedience enables us to imitate Christ's self-giving love, his rejection of "selfish love for oneself."[50] In order to love others and obey God's law, we must "humbly and patiently endure every sort of labor and slander."[51] God's law demands that we love our neighbor, which cannot be done if we hate those who have harmed us.

Some believers will wish to follow a more radical form of obedience, going beyond "ordinary obedience to the Law's commandments."[52] The "counsel" of obedience involves giving up entirely one's self-will, usually by entering a religious order. Such persons, God tells Catherine, walk "[b]y the light of most holy faith, for by this light they will know that they must slay their selfish will with the knife of contempt for every selfish sensual passion and espouse the bride charity will give them," namely "true ready obedience" sustained by patience, humility, and contempt for the world's riches and honors.[53]

Already in this life, when we possess faith, hope, and charity, we receive a "foretaste of eternal life because our will has been clothed in the dear will of God."[54] In faith, we hope not in ourselves but in the God whom we love. A foretaste of hell is to rely on ourselves, since we do not have the power to fulfill even the selfish wishes that we have. Catherine observes, "In fact, when we want to be rich, it often happens that we have to be poor. We would like health and long life, but we have to be sick and time runs out for us ... If we choose to trust in human beings, therefore, we will always be left disillusioned, since we are putting our faith in nothingness."[55] Elizabeth of the Trinity teaches that the life of Christian virtue constitutes a participation in eternal life even now. Even now Jesus Christ has united us to himself through faith and the sacraments of faith. God's kingdom is already within us; Christ lives in us. Of the soul that is being perfected in virtue, Elizabeth says, "The more it is tried, the more its faith increases because it passes over all obstacles, as it were, to go rest in the heart of infinite Love who can

---

[50] Ibid., p. 329.
[51] Ibid., p. 330.
[52] Ibid., p. 334.
[53] Ibid., p. 340.
[54] Catherine of Siena, *The Letters of Catherine of Siena*, Vol. 3, p. 199.
[55] Ibid., pp. 198–9.

perform only works of love."[56] The foretaste of eternal life leads the charitable person to long for beatific union with God the Trinity. As Hadewijch puts it, "But he who is ardent for the sake of Love/Shall yet understand/How Love is always possessed in violent longing:/ Here one cannot find repose."[57]

Conclusion

United to God by faith in Jesus Christ and hoping to share in his glory, we are transformed by charity, which focuse our heart upon God rather than upon earthly goods. In charity we love God as our end, and charity guides the other virtues such as humility, detachment, obedience, justice, fortitude, temperance, patience and so forth. The gifts of the Holy Spirit elevate our minds and hearts to live in accord with the Holy Spirit's promptings. Indeed, the Christian life of virtue is such that eternal life already begins here and now, insofar as it is the indwelling Trinity who makes us holy. Having put on the full armor of God, we can obey God's will with humility rather than rebelling against God through pride. Abandoning ourselves to God's providential care, we can patiently endure adversity without becoming bitter toward God and neighbor. Despite the temptations of power, wealth, and sexual pleasure, we can refuse to use others and instead can learn to give until it hurts. As Catherine urges Cardinal Pietro di Luna, "Think not of yourself but only of Christ crucified. Take your place at the table of the cross and there take souls as your food for God's honor, by suffering with true patience even to the point of death."[58] The virtues enable us to take our place "at the table of the cross."

---

[56] Elizabeth of the Trinity, *Complete Works*, Vol. 1, p. 102.
[57] Hadewijch, *The Complete Works*, p. 181.
[58] Catherine of Siena, *The Letters of Catherine of Siena*, Vol. 3, p. 129.

8

Mary and the saints

Let us begin with the Virgin Mary, and then turn to other saints venerated by the Church. Elizabeth Ann Seton points out that Jesus' nine months in Mary's womb cannot simply be understood as a physical event. There must also have been a spiritual connection. A mother of five children herself, Elizabeth knew that childbearing means an intimate physical and psychological connection between mother and child. Elizabeth describes Mary as Jesus' "tabernacle" during these nine months.[1] Elizabeth also notes that Mary followed Jesus on his path of suffering, all the way to the foot of the Cross. The Incarnation cannot be thought without Mary who bears Jesus in her womb; nor can the Cross be thought without Mary who suffers at the foot of the Cross. Mary cannot be cast aside so as to focus on Jesus.

Elizabeth marvels at the bodily connection between Mary and Jesus. What a privilege it was to be the Mother of God! When we think about the love of a child for his parents, and the love of a mother for her child, we appreciate the incredible dignity that the creature Mary received, and her unique bond with Jesus. In her notes for the Feast of the Assumption, Elizabeth observes, "God taking flesh from her, bone of her bone, flesh of her flesh, blood of her blood, the same which we now adore in our Jesus; in Jesus, our redemption; in Jesus, glorified at the right hand; in Jesus, received in the Eucharist."[2] God prepared his creature Mary to be the one from whom Jesus would receive his bodily nature. Simeon's prophecy

---

[1] Elizabeth Ann Seton, *Elizabeth Ann Seton: A Woman of Prayer: Meditations, Reflections, Prayers and Poems Taken from Her Writings*, ed. Marie Celeste, S. C. (New York: Alba House, 1993), p. 80.

[2] Ibid., p. 82.

revealed to her "the mystery of the salvation and reprobation of the world."[3]

How could she bear the intensity of being the mother of such a child? The only way that she could have faithfully undergone with Jesus the mysteries of his life is if she too was prepared in sanctity to obey God's will. Elizabeth speaks of Mary's happiness even during "the sufferings and ignominies of her son," a happiness made possible by "her full conformity to Him" through the grace of the Holy Spirit that enriched her.[4] Elizabeth also praises Earth as happy in having possessed a mere creature such as Mary, who has a relationship to her child (her Creator) of unique and enduring intimacy. In the writings of Juana Inés de la Cruz, we already observed this perspective on Mary's dignity as the greatest of mere creatures.

Mary's mission, like Jesus', is inseparable from her suffering—in her case the suffering that she endures at the foot of the Cross. Jesus alone redeems us, but all other Christians are called to share in his Cross so as to share in his Resurrection, and Mary is first among Christians. Her compassion, her suffering with Jesus, goes beyond the compassion of any other mere human. Jesus suffers out of love for all of us; Mary unites her sufferings with his in the highest manner. Her compassion extends not only to her son Jesus but to all who are sons and daughters in the Son. She is Jesus' mother in love and compassion, and she therefore becomes our mother in love and compassion. Jesus permits Julian of Norwich, in a mystical vision, to experience something of his own sufferings on the Cross. In Julian's mystical vision she sees that "Christ and she [Mary] were so united in love that the greatness of her love was the cause of the greatness of her pain. For her pain surpassed that of all others, as much as she loved him more than all others."[5]

How do we know that Mary's love and suffering were greater than, for example, John's, who was also at the foot of the Cross and who was Jesus' beloved disciple? Julian grants that "all his disciples and all his true lovers suffered greater pains [at Jesus' death] than they did at the death of their own bodies. For I am sure, by my own

---

[3] Ibid., p. 81.
[4] Ibid.
[5] Julian of Norwich, *Showings*, p. 142.

experience, that the least of them loved him more than they loved themselves."[6] Thus it is not a competition between Mary and other believers. Yet Julian is unwilling to suppose that being the mother of Jesus counts for nothing in terms of Mary's relationship with him (and with all those whom he loves). Mary loves Jesus as the beloved disciple does, but she also loves Jesus with the unique love of a mother. Mary's maternity cannot be separated from the fullness of her unique relationship with her Son.

Furthermore, the mother of the Savior has a maternal relationship to those who are saved. From the Cross, Jesus instructs the beloved disciple to receive her as mother. All disciples of Jesus have Mary truly as their mother, and thus as one who deeply cares for and prays for each of us, with supplications greater than those that Monica made on behalf of her son Augustine. Julian states: "So our Lady is our mother, in whom we are all enclosed and born of her in Christ, for she who is mother of our saviour is mother of all who are saved in our saviour."[7]

Julian has another vision in which Jesus, responding to her wishes, shows her Mary. Mary had previously seemed to Julian to be "small and simple."[8] Mary is indeed small and simple, but now Julian sees her in another way: "now he [Jesus] showed her high and noble and glorious and more pleasing to him than all creatures."[9] She is the greatest creature because, by the grace of the Holy Spirit, her humility and charity are the greatest among mere creatures. She is glorious because she is lowly. To see her only as lowly, as is the case when her glorious Assumption is unrecognized, mistakes who she actually is. Julian observes that Mary now lives "in delight, honour and joy."[10] After seeing Mary's humility and glory, Julian sees Jesus more clearly, so that Jesus tells her, "I am he who is highest. I am he whom you love. I am he in whom you delight. I am he whom you serve. I am he for whom you long. I am he whom you desire. I am he whom you intend."[11]

---

[6] Ibid.
[7] Ibid., p. 292.
[8] Ibid., p. 147.
[9] Ibid.
[10] Ibid.
[11] Ibid.

Julian learns the purpose of Jesus' love for Mary. Jesus explains, "It is for love of you that I have made her so exalted, so noble, so honourable; and this delights me."[12] The love that Jesus has for all his members is the reason for his exaltation of his mother. How could this be so? It would seem that his exalting his mother would make the rest of us jealous and would divert attention from himself. In Mary's exaltation, however, Jesus reveals the goal of the Incarnation, namely his intimacy with the human race. Mary's blessedness shows Jesus' delight in those whom he has come to save. Those who delight in Jesus will delight, as he does, in Mary. Julian says that it is "as if, when a man loves some creature particularly more than all other creatures, he will make all other creatures to love and delight in that creature whom he loves so much."[13]

In her mystical vision of the symphony of the blessed, Hildegard of Bingen similarly sees Mary receiving praise from all creation. The saints and angels praise Mary: "He formed the Word in you as a human being,/And therefore you are the jewel that shines most brightly."[14] The image of glorified creation as a treasury of jewels helps us to understand Mary's place. All the saints and angels are God's beautiful "jewels;" they are the most beautiful and valuable creatures that God has made. Like jewels, they shine not with their own inner illumination, but from an exterior light. Among these jewels, Mary "shines most brightly" because she received the Word into her womb. This could not have happened unless her soul had been as translucent to the Word as was her body. In Hildegard's vision, therefore, the saints and angels extol her as "serenely infused with the Sun."[15] To some degree, we have lost this sense for what is beautiful in God's creation. Hildegard recognizes that the most beautiful mere creature is Mary, whose face reflects fully the face of Jesus.

Mechthild of Magdeburg imagines that Mary and Joseph were quite poor, so that Joseph had to work hard as a carpenter and Mary had to work hard providing for the needs of the family. Yet had Mary not been spiritually rich, she would have been shamed

---

[12] Ibid., p. 222.
[13] Ibid., p. 223.
[14] Hildegard of Bingen, *Scivias*, p. 525.
[15] Ibid.

by the purity of the angel Gabriel. Even prior to the annunciation, Mary's prayers could not have been meager. She must have been prepared spiritually to receive the Son of God. Mechthild says of Mary, "Looking at the angel she discovered in his face the same chasteness that she had. She stood there with great composure, inclined her ear, and raised up her mind. Then the angel greeted her and announced God's will to her. His words were pleasing to her heart; her senses became full and her soul fiery."[16] Her "fiery" soul, bright with the grace of the Holy Spirit, enables her to accept the vocation of being the mother of the crucified Lord and our mother. She can only do this if she has marvelous love.

It is this love that undergirds her glorious kinship with Jesus. Mechthild describes the Incarnation in such a way as to emphasize the primacy of love in the physical event: God "passed through her whole virginal body into the fiery soul of her devout will, placed itself in the open heart of her most pure flesh, and united itself with all that it found in her, so that her flesh became its flesh in such a manner that a perfect child grew in her body and she became a true mother of his flesh."[17] Carrying the infant Jesus in her womb was both a bodily and a spiritual experience for Mary. To emphasize this, Mechthild imagines that the pregnant Mary not only became great with child, but also at the same time increased in radiance, beauty, and wisdom.

As an example of Mary's fiery love, Mechthild points out that Joseph and Mary do not seem to have benefited financially from the gifts of gold, frankincense, and myrrh that the baby Jesus received from the three wise men from the East. We read in the Gospel of Luke that Joseph and Mary could afford only a pair of turtledoves or pigeons when they presented Jesus to be circumcised in the Temple. According to Mechthild's vision, Mary explains that she already knew that her sacrificial lamb was Jesus himself. Mary tells Mechthild, "The offerings that were brought to my Child I used to remember all those whom I found truly to be in need. These were poor orphans, and pure virgins who were thereby able to marry and not be stoned. Also, those who were alone and those far advanced in age: these were supposed to have the advantage of it."[18]

---

[16] Mechthild of Magdeburg, *The Flowing Light of the Godhead*, trans. Frank Tobin (New York: Paulist Press, 1998), p. 198.

[17] Ibid.

Louise de Marillac argues that God's grace defines Mary so fully that "[s]he was saved without ever having been lost."[19] Did God save her, then, with no reference to the salvation accomplished by Christ? No, because God saved her from all sin precisely in his knowledge that she was to be the mother of Christ. She was saved through the merits of Christ, so as to be part of making those merits possible. She had to be able to consent with perfect freedom to the vocation of bearing Christ. Her glorious vocation reflects God's glorious generosity. He ensured that she dwelt fully in her Son, just as her Son dwelt in her womb and in her home. Angela of Foligno remarks in this vein: "The mother of God was adorned with privileges and virtues so unique, and with gifts so ineffable, that nothing could separate her, not even for a moment, from divine union."[20] God's gifts ensured that her bodily motherhood was not discordant with her spiritual condition.

Birgitta of Sweden ties together Mary's immaculate conception with Mary's bodily Assumption. Both have to do with the generosity and justice of the Son of God. Due to her perfect love for him from the annunciation through his Pasch, Jesus rewarded her by restoring to her the body in which he had dwelt for nine months. Birgitta praises her, "You merited to see your body revived after your death and assumed with your soul into heaven amidst honor from the angels. You acknowledged that your glorious Son was God with a human nature; and with exultant joy, you saw that he is the most just judge of all and the rewarder of good works."[21] These good works came from the grace of the Holy Spirit who prepared and sustained Mary for her vocation as mother of her Savior. Due to this grace, Mary's body not only carried Jesus physically, but was also free from any taint arising from spiritual sin. Her bodily actions on earth, like her spiritual actions, were performed "with such charity that God, in justice, had to revere it [her body] with highest honor."[22]

Mary's bodily Assumption into heaven, like her immaculate conception, belongs to her unique vocation of love. As Birgitta says to Mary, "Your flesh then understood that the more ardently that

---

[18] Ibid., p. 201.
[19] Louise de Marillac, *Writings*, p. 229.
[20] Angela of Foligno, *Complete Works*, p. 238.
[21] Birgitta of Sweden, *Life and Selected Revelations*, p. 225.
[22] Ibid.

anyone loves God in this world, the nearer to himself will God place that person in heaven."[23] Configured supremely to the Son whose temple her body was, Mary's love is such that she receives not merely a spiritual reward but a bodily reward. Those who love Jesus rejoice at this reward, because they see its supreme justice and goodness within the order of love. Birgitta concludes, "For it was manifestly clear to the whole court of heaven that no angel and no human loved God with such charity as you did; and therefore it was right and just that with honor God himself placed you, body and soul, on the highest seat of glory."[24]

The new Adam, exalted to the right hand of the Father, has called the new Eve to his side. Teresa of Avila states that on the Feast of the Assumption of Mary, she had an experience of rapture in which God "showed me her [Mary's] ascent to heaven, the happiness and solemnity with which she was received, and the place where she is."[25] Elisabeth of Schönau had a similar experience on the Feast of the Assumption of Mary.[26] The new Eve already sits together with the new Adam, so that the redemption of the human race has truly begun. Mary sits with Jesus the King. Her ongoing relationship with Jesus is filled with love for her Savior and for all whom he has redeemed, who are sons and daughters in her Son. Put another way, Jesus even now inspires Mary, as he inspires all believers, to pray for her neighbors; and Mary does so with marvelous love because of her supreme love for her Son. So as to build up his body the Church as a communion of love, Jesus wills both that we pray to him directly and that we also depend on our friends (and his) for their prayers. Chief among his friends is Mary, who is closest to him in love. In this respect, Birgitta remarks that "for all sinners you [Mary] stand forth as a most faithful advocate and proxy."[27]

Why would we need an "advocate and proxy" with our beloved Jesus? The answer, again, has to do with the Church as a communion of love. Jesus, who died for our sins and poured forth the Holy Spirit, requires us to relate to him not as isolated individuals but as members of his body. When we share in his love, we pray for the

---

[23] Ibid.
[24] Ibid.
[25] Teresa of Avila, *The Collected Works of St. Teresa of Avila*, Vol. 1, p. 276.
[26] Elisabeth of Schönau, *The Complete Works*, p. 209.
[27] Ibid.

whole communion of his members (and potential members), and his members in turn pray for us. Those who have died in Christ, such as Mary, belong to this circle of prayer. Since Mary's love is so rich, her prayer for all those for whom Jesus died is so rich. Although Jesus could meet our needs without the prayers of his friends, he wills to love us within the communion of love and prayer in which Mary plays an important role.

All humans are called to join as saints in this communion of supreme love for God and neighbor. Thérèse of Lisieux remarks in this regard that "I have always wanted to be a saint," but she immediately adds, "Alas! I have always noticed that when I compared myself to the saints, there is between them and me the same difference that exists between a mountain whose summit is lost in the clouds and the obscure grain of sand trampled underfoot by passers-by."[28] Yet she does not therefore lose hope, because her hope is in God, and "God cannot inspire unrealizable desires."[29] Even the littlest believer can become a saint. Recognizing herself as little, she observes that there must then be a "little way" to the sanctity and union with God that she desires. The little way that she needs must be an "elevator," because she does not trust herself to be able to make a steep ascent.[30]

Jesus himself is this "elevator:" he offers to raise us to himself in his own arms, and he can do so only if we remain as spiritual children, dependent on him for everything. She can thus become a saint precisely by remaining "little," indeed by becoming ever more "little." Her experience of accepting, by God's grace, the little sufferings of daily life makes her sufficiently little—through victories of love—to undergo the increasing littleness that is the path of mortal illness. On this path, she says, "Jesus does not want me to lay claim to what belongs to me; and this should seem easy and natural to me since *nothing is mine*."[31] Instead, what she must possess is love, and she must share this with others without hoping for an earthly return.

---

[28] Thérèse of Lisieux, *Story of a Soul*, p. 207.
[29] Ibid.
[30] Ibid.
[31] Ibid., 226.

Thérèse experiences the presence of the saints who have died and now live with God. She speaks of one such experience: "I *believed*, I *felt* there was a *heaven* and that this *heaven* is people with souls who actually love me, who consider me their child."[32] Similarly, she has an encounter, in a dream, with the foundress of the Carmelites in France, Anne de Lobera, a companion of Teresa of Avila. In her dream "the tallest of the saints advanced toward me; immediately I fell to my knees. Oh! what happiness! the Carmelite *raised her veil or rather she raised it and covered me with it*." Recognizing Anne, Thérèse sees that Anne's greatness lay in her translucence to God: "I saw this heavenly face suffused with an unspeakably gentle light, a light it didn't receive from without but was produced from within."[33] Anne promises Thérèse that God will soon come to usher Thérèse from this life into eternal life.

Within a few months of her death, Thérèse told her Carmelite sisters, "I feel that my mission is about to begin, my mission of making others love God as I love Him, my mission of teaching my little way to souls. If God answers my requests, my heaven will be spent on earth up until the end of the world. Yes, I want to spend my heaven doing good on earth."[34] In her book, she describes her sense of mission. She has the ambition to serve God powerfully in every way: as Carmelite, mother of souls, spouse of Christ, priest, apostle, teacher, martyr, crusader. She wants to be at the forefront of every vocation, and to give her life in an extraordinary way for Jesus. She wants to perform the actions of every saint. She pokes fun at herself because she would not even be satisfied by merely one form of martyrdom: "Like You, my Adorable Spouse, I would be scourged and crucified. I would die flayed like St. Bartholomew. I would be plunged into boiling oil like St. John."[35] How can such extraordinary ambition be satisfied? She finds an answer in the Apostle Paul. After listing various vocations, Paul urges the Corinthians to "earnestly desire the higher gifts. And I will show you a still more excellent way" (1 Cor. 12.31), namely the way of love. The one who has love shares in every vocation. Here is how Thérèse describes it: "*I understand it was Love alone* that made the

---

32 Ibid., p. 190.
33 Ibid., p. 191.
34 Ibid., p. 263.
35 Ibid., p. 193.

Church's members act, that if *Love* ever became extinct, apostles would not preach the Gospel and martyrs would not shed their blood. I understand that LOVE COMPRISED ALL VOCATIONS, THAT LOVE WAS EVERYTHING."[36]

True ambition, then, consists in the ambition to love. Love is true greatness even while also being true littleness. Thérèse begs the angels and saints to adopt her as their child in the heavenly communion of love. She sees herself as a little child in the midst of the Church's mature saints, in whose company she hopes to be. Since they are glorified, they already share in the fullness of divine love. The extent of this love awes and almost overwhelms Thérèse. She asks Jesus: "How can a soul as imperfect as mine aspire to the possession of the plenitude of *Love*? O Jesus, *my first and only Friend*, you whom *I love* UNIQUELY, explain this mystery to me!"[37] How is it, in other words, that she dares to claim and to desire real friendship with Jesus in his divine love?

In answer, she offers an image: Jesus is the Eagle who carries us to "the Divine Furnace of the Holy Trinity," a furnace of love. We are only weak little birds; we desire to fly toward this Sun, but we can barely raise our wings. We wish to imitate our brothers and sisters the eagles, that is, the saints who have received the power to fly with Jesus. The danger is that "being unable to soar like the eagles, the poor little bird is taken up with the trifles of earth."[38] Rather than losing the desire to fly toward divine Love, however, we should come again to the Sun, in repentance and in trust. The Eagle unites us to himself in the Eucharist, and we ascend with him "to the bosom of the Eternal Fire of the Blessed Trinity."[39] In love with the "Eagle," we do not ignore the "eagles" who are the saints; rather we ask for their prayers so that we can fly with them in the unity of the bride, the Church. The wings with which all of us fly are Jesus'.

Angela of Foligno relates an experience that shows how when we appeal to the saints, their prayers for us draw us closer to God. As wise and loving friends, they do not tie us to themselves but instead help us journey toward God. In prayer, Angela asks St. Francis that

---

[36] Ibid., p. 194.
[37] Ibid., p. 197.
[38] Ibid., p. 198.
[39] Ibid., p. 199.

he obtain for her certain "graces from the Lord Jesus Christ."[40] She then receives a mystical vision in which the Holy Spirit comes to her and consoles her with the divine presence. The Holy Spirit tells her to imitate St. Francis: "You prayed to my servant Francis and because my servant Francis loved me very much, I, therefore, did much for him. And if there was any other person who loved me still more, I would do even more for him. And I will do for you what I did for my servant Francis, and more if you love me."[41] This episode shows the purpose of asking the saints to intercede for us. We have a direct relationship with Jesus and the Holy Spirit, but we have this relationship within the communion of love that is the Church, whose most loving members are the saints.

After their deaths on earth, Mary and the other saints do not lose their vocation of love for God and neighbor. Rather, this vocation can only be intensified, because the Church is one communion of love. In this light, Elisabeth of Schönau portrays her own prayers as acts of entering into the communion of love enjoyed by the saints who see Jesus. Her prayers are efficacious insofar as they belong to this entire communion of prayer. For example, seeking to grow in holiness, she asks for the aid of Mary and the apostles, whom she sees in a mystical vision. An angel also helps her, just as angels helped Christ and the apostles.[42] In another mystical vision, Elisabeth sees "many thousands of crowned saints—I reckon more than one hundred and forty-four thousand—who were all crowned with golden crowns."[43] These visions, when combined with her mystical communion with Jesus in the Eucharist, inspire her to share with others the truth that life eternal is real and awaits us if we grow in love.

Conclusion

Comprised of angels and humans, the Church is a communion of love gathered around the one mediator Jesus Christ, who enables

---

[40] Angela of Foligno, *Complete Works*, p. 139.
[41] Ibid., p. 140.
[42] See Elisabeth of Schönau, *The Complete Works*, pp. 92–3.
[43] Ibid., p. 78.

us to share in the eternal love of the Father and the Son in the Holy Spirit. Death does not sever people from the Church. The mission of the saints on behalf of all humanity continues until the end of the world. As the Mother of God, Mary is foremost among the saints. In giving birth to Love incarnate, she participates with unique closeness in his love. Because she is his mother, she is the mother of all who are sons and daughters in the Son. Nor is Jesus' love for her separable from love for her flesh, which was truly the temple of God. In Mary, the Church already takes her place in the wedding feast of heaven. The communion of love is growing day by day, due to the love Jesus has for his people and to the love and prayers that his people, sharing in his Spirit, lift up to him on behalf of the human race. God calls us today to join in this communion of love, in which we commune directly with Jesus with the help of his beloved friends and servants.

9

Prayer

Teresa of Avila wrote *The Way of Perfection* for her Carmelite sisters. At the outset, she points out that the Carmelites enjoy an advantage in prayer that those in the world do not possess, namely the ability to focus their lives on prayer. One role of prayer is to keep us from cleaving to the world as though it were our permanent home. To follow Jesus, we need to be "interiorly fortified through an understanding of the importance of trampling everything underfoot, of detachment from things that come to an end, and of attachment to eternal things."[1] We must continually renew our relationship with God through prayer. This is no less true for people in the world than for cloistered religious sisters, even though the latter have the responsibility of working hard at prayer so as (among other things) to strengthen those in the world.

To pray well, we must be prepared by love, detachment, and humility. We should also regularly receive the sacrament of reconciliation and listen to the advice of our confessor. We must desire to love, rather than wishing above all to be loved. We should not find our supreme solace in the things of this world or focus ourselves on our bodily health and comfort. We can hardly be humble if we are centered on ourselves, our privileges, and our reputation. If we are to pray well, then we should be willing to follow Jesus on the path of the Cross. When we are loving, detached, and humble, we have the openness to God and desire for God that foster true prayer.

Teresa goes on to speak of vocal prayer, mental prayer, and contemplation. Vocal prayer is joined to mental prayer when we are focused not on the words of the prayers that we are saying,

---

[1] Teresa of Avila, *The Collected Works of St. Teresa of Avila*, Vol. 2, trans. Kieran Kavanaugh, O. C. D., and Otilio Rodriguez, O. C. D. (Washington, D.C.: ICS Publications, 1980), p. 49.

but on the presence of God to whom we speak the words. Often, she recognizes, we can be speaking the words and thinking about worldly things; in this case we are far from mental prayer. What is needed is that before saying our vocal prayers (e.g. the rosary), we think about "whom we are going to speak with, and who we are."[2] When we recognize that we are mere mortals who are going to speak to the infinite God, we will be much more likely to truly speak with God in vocal prayer rather than merely saying the words while thinking about something else. Teresa urges us not to act rudely toward God by ignoring him while speaking to him in vocal prayer. Instead, we should engage in mental prayer via vocal prayer.

By giving us the Lord's Prayer, Jesus made clear that doing without vocal prayer is not an option for Christians. When Jesus prayed vocally, he usually did so in solitude. Teresa understands this to be an example for us. We too should recite our vocal prayers in solitude so as to concentrate all our attention on what we are saying and to whom we are saying it. Even in solitude, of course, we can still be beset by distractions. In such cases, we should generally keep praying, although sometimes we should simply turn our attention to other works of virtue. When we say the Lord's Prayer, we should remember that the one who taught us this prayer is with us, and we should concentrate upon being in his presence. To prepare for vocal prayer, we must examine our conscience, make an act of contrition, and make the sign of the cross. We should be aware that Jesus is with us in our solitude.

When we are undertaking vocal prayer with the goal that it also be mental prayer, we need first to learn how to quiet our minds so that we will not be distracted by other thoughts. Teresa admits that for many years she had great difficulty in quieting her mind. The key is to persevere in striving to place ourselves in the presence of Jesus. This does not mean merely thinking about Jesus. Rather, we should try to direct the eye of our mind toward Jesus, to look at him. Even if we can only do this for a short period, he will return our gaze and will strengthen our focus. We should use our imagination in looking at Jesus. When we are joyful, we should look on him as the risen one; when we are sorrowful, we should look on him as he

---

[2] Ibid., p. 123.

walks to the Garden of Gethsemane or endures scourging and the Cross. By looking at him in this manner, we will be able to focus on uniting ourselves with him and we will turn away from distracting thoughts.

These efforts will bear fruit in mental prayer and recollection. In recollection, "the soul collects its faculties together and enters within itself to be with its God."[3] The deepest form of recollection is God's gift rather than our work. Teresa cautions, "Don't think this recollection is acquired by the intellect striving to think about God within itself, or by the imagination imagining Him within itself."[4] Describing the varying degrees of recollection, Teresa uses the image of moving away from land and traveling by sea. The "land" consists in the thoughts and images that stimulate our mind; whereas in recollection we enter into ourselves so as no longer to rely so much on the things of this world. She explains that recollection is so valuable because it enables us to be more quickly ignited by "the fire of divine love."[5] We find ourselves in the presence of God alone, freed from outside impediments.

As an entrance point into prayer, Teresa recommends meditation. Meditation involves thinking about spiritual matters, often by reading Scripture or devotional books. She advises using "a good book written in the vernacular in order to recollect one's thoughts and pray well vocally, and little by little accustom the soul with coaxing and skill not to grow discouraged."[6] During meditation, we should frequently break off our train of thought to devote ourselves to "making acts of love, praising God, rejoicing in His goodness, that He is who He is, and in desiring His honor and glory."[7] In other words, we should combine the intellectual work of meditation with efforts to inspire our will to proper devotion. We need both intellect and will to be fully engaged in the labor of vocal and mental prayer. Indeed, union with God through prayer is fueled more by love than by intellect, although the latter has a role. Even when we are recollected in prayer, it may be that our imagination continues to stray due to headaches and other such troubles; but

---

[3] Ibid., p. 141.
[4] Ibid., p. 328.
[5] Ibid., p. 143.
[6] Ibid., p. 136.
[7] Ibid., p. 319.

so long as our intellect and will are focused on God, we should not allow a wayward imagination to alarm us.

Teresa thinks that when vocal prayer is also mental prayer, it can be the occasion of the gift of contemplation. In contemplation, our intellect no longer has the leading role. Instead, God "speaks to the soul" directly.[8] God binds our intellect and imagination so that we cannot speak. Contemplation can be prepared for, but we are not in charge of it. God gives it to us as a grace. She explains, "The soul understands that without the noise of words this divine Master is teaching it by suspending its faculties, for if they were to be at work they would do harm rather than bring benefit."[9] Our concepts and images could only get in the way of the intimacy that God desires to give us through contemplation. Rather than thinking conceptually about what God is communicating to us, we are able simply to enjoy it. God inflames us with love and we know that we are loving, but we do not understand how we are loving and enjoying God. Instead we experience a love and joy that is above our understanding because utterly above our nature. When the period of contemplation comes to an end, we are able to understand it insofar as we recognize that God has given us a wondrous gift that we could not have merited. Whereas in vocal prayer and mental prayer we are at work, we do nothing in contemplation other than receive what God does for us.

We can prepare for contemplation by working hard to gain the virtues. Possessing virtue to a high degree prepares the soul for contemplation, just as possessing virtue is of value for mental prayer. In Teresa's own case, she says that it took her twenty years of mental prayer and laborious efforts to gain virtue before she received the gift of contemplation. Yet God sometimes gives the gift of contemplation to persons who are unprepared, so as to encourage them and convert them. As Teresa says, God "even places them in contemplation sometimes, though He does so rarely and it lasts only a short while."[10] This underscores that contemplation is purely God's gift rather than something we can manipulate. We must not become frustrated if we cultivate mental prayer and the virtues for years without receiving the gift of contemplation, while others who seem unworthy receive the gift of contemplation all at once.

---

[8] Ibid., p. 131.
[9] Ibid.
[10] Ibid., p. 96.

When finally we receive contemplation, Teresa thinks that God will continue to bestow it upon us regularly, unless we fail to continue preparing for it. If we slacken our efforts to give ourselves to God, God will stimulate our desire for him "by leaving us in mental prayer and visiting us from time to time like servants in His vineyard."[11] Once we have first received contemplation, we will continue to receive it so long as we continue to prepare assiduously for it. In this state, God cares for us as his beloved children, so that (as Teresa puts it) we dine at his table and share in his food. At the highest stages of the spiritual life, however, contemplation may be withheld along with other consolations so as to purify us.

What about those who never receive contemplation? On the one hand, Teresa urges everyone to prepare "so that God may lead you along this path if He so desires."[12] But on the other hand, those whom God does not lead along the path of contemplation have the opportunity to practice greater humility. By no means should they view themselves as less loved by God. On the contrary, God may simply be increasing their humility. They may be walking on the highest path, even though they lack the experience of contemplation. Teresa emphasizes in this regard that "God doesn't lead all by one path, and perhaps the one who thinks she is walking along a very lowly path is in fact higher in the eyes of the Lord."[13] It would be impossible, in Teresa's view, for everyone at a particular Carmel to be a contemplative. Yet if we continue diligently in mental prayer, God can give us contemplation when we least expect it. We should not fear that receiving contemplation will puff us up with pride. If the delight that we experience in contemplation is from God, the experience will in fact strengthen our humility.

Even as we try to advance in prayer, we should keep in view that the Lord, not we ourselves, will choose the path by which we can best attain to him. Nonetheless, we should not use this fact as an excuse not to try to prepare ourselves for contemplation. Teresa believes that almost all who persevere and who are humble and detached will receive contemplation; the very few exceptions have been chosen by God to receive it "all at once in heaven," since they

---

[11] Ibid., p. 97.
[12] Ibid., p. 99.
[13] Ibid.

have followed the path of the Cross here on earth.[14] She emphasizes that although God has provided many paths of prayer, God calls all people to contemplation in the sense of not excluding anyone from contemplation. God wishes for perseverance and determination on our part. Even if we give up before we receive contemplation, we still benefit spiritually from our efforts to seek the gift of contemplation.

Given that contemplation is so joyful, is it an easier path than mental prayer? Teresa says that contemplation involves many trials. The delight of contemplation is necessary because otherwise its trials would be too hard to bear. According to Teresa, God leads contemplatives "along a rough and uneven path and at times they think they are lost and must return to begin again."[15] Considering ourselves weak, we may be tempted to avoid the quest for contemplation, but God will give us courage if we desire it. Such courage especially comes into play in renouncing our own will. In order to avoid the danger of pride, contemplatives must practice obedience to others. Those who wish to be contemplatives must endure the mortification of handing over their will to a carefully chosen confessor.

By giving us the gift of contemplation, God gives us the "living water" that refreshes, cleanses, and satisfies us. When we are tired of the world and can barely endure earthly life's ongoing deprivation of God's presence, so that we might even die of love, God comes to our assistance by means of the living water of contemplation. In this way God enables the soul "to enjoy what in herself she couldn't without dying."[16] Rather than being a flight from the world, contemplation is what sustains us in earthly life. Contemplation both makes it possible to go on living—rather than dying of love for the God whose full presence we desire—and inspires the human race by highlighting the purpose of living, namely union with God. As Teresa puts it somewhat paradoxically, "[P]erhaps by continuing to live we can help others die of desire for this death."[17]

She warns that Satan can tempt contemplatives to overdo bodily penances and ruin their health. Like St. Paul, contemplatives will

---

[14] Ibid., p. 101.
[15] Ibid., p. 102.
[16] Ibid., p. 111.
[17] Ibid.

experience a strong desire to die and be with God. They must firmly
resist doing any penances that will tend in this direction. In this
sense, they must even mortify their desire to be with God, when
they sense that this desire would otherwise cause them to die. They
should fear that such a powerful desire may be from Satan rather
than from God. In such cases they should mortify their desire to die,
"even though the experience may [in fact] come from the Spirit of
God."[18] They should reflect on the fact that by continuing to live on
this earth, they may "serve God more and enlighten some soul that
would have been lost" and may also, through this service, merit to
enjoy God more in eternal life.[19] In this regard, Teresa recalls John
Cassian's story about the monk who, tempted by the devil, came to
"think that by throwing himself into a well he would see God more
quickly."[20] Adding that God would not have allowed the monk to
do such a thing had the monk not already turned away from God,
she reiterates that if contemplatives experience signs that they are
harming their health, they need to shorten even the most delightful
time of prayer, no matter how painful it is to do this.

Although Teresa affirms that all believers must pray, the degrees
of perfection in prayer may make prayer seem to be primarily for an
elite. Teresa insists, however, that because God "loves us He adapts
Himself to our size."[21] Prayer is not a competition with others. The
main goal, after all, is to increase in love, detachment, and humility,
because these are at the center of our relationship with God. As
Teresa puts it, "If contemplating, practicing mental and vocal prayer,
taking care of the sick, helping with household chores, and working
even at the lowliest tasks are all ways of serving the Guest who
comes to be with us and eat and recreate, what difference does it
make whether we serve in one way or the other?"[22] In addition, no
matter how advanced in prayer we become, we should not abandon
frequently praying together in community.

When we persist in prayer, God will assist us in giving ourselves
to him. We need not fear to receive the infinitely great God into
our small souls. God will gradually increase our spiritual capacity

---

[18] Ibid., 112.
[19] Ibid.
[20] Ibid., p. 113.
[21] Ibid., p. 144.
[22] Ibid., p. 101.

until we can receive him in earnest. Teresa explains that "since He doesn't force our will, He takes what we give Him; but He doesn't give Himself completely until we give ourselves completely."[23] Nor does God come alone; he intends for us to receive all who love him. When we open our souls to God, we commune not only with God but also with all his holy angels and saints in their supreme charity. Far from envying God's love for us, they rejoice in it, so that prayer is never a competitive or solitary experience. Yet our primary communion is always with our divine Spouse, whose love we enjoy as though in "solitude."[24]

It may seem that Teresa's depiction of contemplation puts vocal prayer entirely in the shade. With contemplation in view, however, Teresa rejoices in the Lord's Prayer. Its first words, "Our Father who art in heaven," suffice for perfect contemplation. She urges us to reflect on what we are saying when we speak of our "Father" and of "heaven." The love that the divine Son shows for us reveals the Father's love, and we should indeed be grateful for having such a generous Father. The fact that this Father dwells in "heaven" should lead us not to fear death but to desire to do everything here on earth so that we might dwell with the Father in heaven. Even the very first words of this vocal prayer, then, "fill our hands and give a reward so large that it would easily fill the intellect and thus occupy the will in such a way one would be unable to speak a word."[25]

The life of prayer is motivated by the fact that the Father cares for us as children. We dare to pray, sinners that we are, because the Father has promised to forgive his prodigal children when we return to him in repentance. Since he is our Father, he will sustain us through the trials that we encounter. Indeed, we can trust him to help us far more than any human father would, because he is perfect love. His goal is not only to build up our relationship with him, but actually to make us sharers of the Son's inheritance. Given this divine love and humility, we have every reason to expect that he will bless our communion with him in prayer. No matter our background or worldly status, we can become great in our Father's house. In this light, Teresa urges us to "find your delight in Him;

[23] Ibid., p. 145.
[24] Ibid., p. 146.
[25] Ibid., p. 137.

and cast yourselves into His arms."[26] We do this by prayer. No wonder then that prayer offers such great delight to those who devote themselves to it.

The relationship that Gertrud the Great has with the Lord in prayer exemplifies this delight. Once during communal prayer, Gertrud prayed for God to bless his people. It seemed to her that in return, God himself asked for her blessing, by which God meant her sincere repentance and desire to avoid sin. When in prayer she made this act of contrition, "the Lord of heaven bowed deeply with joy."[27] Similarly, after being distracted from prayer during an illness, she returned to fervent prayer after her recovery and feared that it would be a struggle. Instead, she "suddenly sensed that the goodness of God was bending toward her in a most alluring embrace and saying, 'Daughter, you are always with me and all that is mine is yours.'"[28] Again, recalling her past sins, she felt downcast and feared to put herself forward, only to experience that "the Lord bent down to her with such courtesy that all the court of heaven, as if astonished, was striving to call him back. To this the Lord replied, 'I cannot possibly restrain myself from pursuing her, for she attracts my divine Heart to her with such powerful cords of humility.'"[29]

At another time, Gertrud in meditation experienced a feeling of profound unworthiness and humiliation. She then had a vision of God, supremely transcendent and supremely loving, giving grace through the heart of Jesus. She received this grace as through a reed. The image is a eucharistic one, evoking the precious blood of Jesus by which God accomplished the salvation of the world. Similarly, Jesus' sacred heart appeared to her in the form of a lamp. She recounts that when she "through recollecting her failings grew humble, the Lord immediately had mercy on her and poured into her from his own most blessed Heart the blossoming spring growth of his own divine virtues."[30]

In these images of God's personal love and tenderness, we see the meaning of Christian prayer. It is a relationship with divine Love, a relationship that overcomes the impediments of our weakness and

---

[26] Ibid., p. 139.
[27] Gertrud the Great of Helfta, *The Herald of God's Loving-Kindness: Book* 3, 109.
[28] Ibid., p. 115.
[29] Ibid., p. 117.
[30] Ibid., p. 95.

sinfulness and that fills us with joy. As Gertrud describes this joy, "Among these most delightful pleasures she perceived that in an inestimably wonderful fashion she was being drawn to the Lord's Heart through the same reed that has been often mentioned."[31] Caught up eucharistically into the heart of Jesus, she experienced a rapturous union with him. This union, an experience of highest contemplation, awakens all the spiritual senses and transcends the conceptual realm. She says that "what she sensed, what she saw, what she heard, what she tasted and what she touched, was known to her alone and to him who deigned to admit her to such a superexcellently sublime union with himself, Jesus the bridegroom of the loving soul, who is God, blessed above all for ever."[32]

Gertrud had many of her most intense encounters with God while praying during or after the rite of the Eucharist. In this way she bears witness to of liturgical prayer for Christians. (Teresa of Avila, too, of course, has intense experiences of prayer centered on the eucharistic liturgy.) Gertrud describes one such experience that happened as she prepared to receive communion. She felt herself "being invited by the Lord in her inmost being, as if she were in the heavenly palace, about to take her seat by God the Father in the kingdom of his glory and eat at his table with him."[33] This disconcerted her because she hardly felt worthy for such extraordinary intimacy with God. The divine Son then came and cleansed her by his Passion, and made her his bride, giving her "his own jewels—necklace, bracelets, and rings."[34] From this experience she learned that God's grace in Christ Jesus is always sufficient to prepare us for divine intimacy. Another time, while participating in the sacrifice of the Mass, she was astonished to discover in prayer that her own prayers had been used by God for the benefit of souls. Yet again, when about to receive communion, she found in prayer that she was becoming more and more united to Jesus' Passion, so that she experienced with increasing devotion the power of his redemptive suffering. After she had received communion and when she was immersed in prayer, Jesus appeared to her in the form of a

---

[31] Ibid., p. 96.
[32] Ibid.
[33] Ibid., p. 79.
[34] Ibid.

pelican, symbolizing his desire to give her eternal life through his own blood.

If prayer is powerful, why does God not always answer the prayers of those whom he loves? Birgitta of Sweden asks God this question. God answers that he knows better than we do what is best for us. Thus we often pray for things that in fact are not for our best welfare. An example of this is St. Paul's prayer that the "thorn" in his flesh be removed. Paul prays three times that God remove this thorn, but God answers him that it is better for the thorn to be there, so as to make clear that God's grace is sufficient despite our weakness and indeed that God's "power is made perfect in weakness" (2 Cor. 12.9). When we pray to be relieved of weakness or illness, or when we pray that others be relieved of such things, God may not answer us because he knows that the weakness or illness actually serves our (or others') good. What appears to us to be God's "indignation" or refusal to answer our prayer is in fact God's great mercy toward those whom he loves.[35] God permits us to be tested by trials in this life, both so that we may merit reward in Christ, and so that our spiritual weaknesses may be healed through purification.

When God leaves prayers unanswered, we often find it hard to accept this. Angela of Foligno cautions in this regard that "[t]here are many who believe themselves to be in a state of love who are actually in a state of hatred."[36] How can we gain insight into our spiritual condition? In our prayer, we need to face the question of whether when we think we are loving God, we are actually loving the good things that God gives us. It may be that we love bodily health and wellbeing more than we love God. Angela describes diseased souls: "They even love material things to put these at the service of the gods they have made of their bodies. They love their friends and relatives inordinately as a way of benefiting from them and being honored by them. They love spiritual persons not for their goodness but to cover themselves with the mantle of holiness."[37] When we get mired in this condition, how can we get out? We can do so by recognizing our profound need for God. Angela urges us to imitate Francis of Assisi, who "near the end of his life, even though

---

[35] Birgitta of Sweden, *Life and Selected Revelations*, p. 145.
[36] Angela of Foligno, *Complete Works*, p. 225.
[37] Ibid.

his state of perfection was so excellent and his union with God so ineffable, nonetheless . . . said: 'Brothers, let us begin to do penance for until now we have made little progress.'"[38] Since we easily cleave to creatures rather than to God, our prayer has to be rooted in a penitential sense of our need for God's help in loving him.

Why worry so much about loving God, when after all he cannot be seen and the things he has created seem good enough in themselves without bringing God into the picture? Angela answers that the key is to discover that "God is indeed the only one who has being, and that nothing has being unless it comes from him."[39] This discovery that we are creatures, and that God is radically not a creature, fuels our quest for the One who loved us into existence. Angela explains, "The soul drawn out of itself and led into this vision derives from it an ineffable wisdom, one that is deep and mature."[40] We discover what it means to say that the Creator is the Redeemer. Angela observes, "When the soul sees the supreme Being stoop down lovingly toward creatures, it does likewise."[41] In love with God, centered on God, we truly become lovers of others, whereas before we had been centered on ourselves.

Writing to her friend Piero Canigiani, Catherine of Siena similarly underscores that "if we love ourselves with a selfish, sensual love, we cannot love either God or ourselves with a reasonable love."[42] We can be blinded by self-centered love. We need to be humble, patient, willing to suffer, and generous in opening our hearts to God and neighbor. Often we are the very opposite. The path of prayer opens us to see reality more clearly and to learn to love, by God's grace, what is truly lovable. Catherine says that "if we set ourselves to getting to know our own poverty and the world's flimsiness, inconstancy, and instability, we will immediately hate these, and so eliminate our love for them."[43] Because we are made to love, we will then begin to love the enduring realities, namely the God who loves us into existence and recreates us by the blood of his own Son. Catherine asks Piero "to strip yourself of yourself and

---

[38] Ibid.
[39] Ibid., p. 227.
[40] Ibid.
[41] Ibid., p. 228.
[42] Catherine of Siena, *The Letters of Catherine of Siena*, Vol. 3, p. 227.
[43] Ibid., pp. 228–9.

to clothe yourself in Christ crucified ... Love! Love! For you are loved indescribably much!"[44] When Catherine herself experiences temptation, she wards it off by confessing her sinfulness and taking refuge in Christ crucified, her Savior.[45] This is the path of prayer. We discover our sinfulness and neediness, and we learn to embrace the Creator God who has reached out in Christ and the Spirit to embrace us in love.

God teaches Catherine that "if she truly perseveres, the soul learns every virtue in constant and faithful humble prayer."[46] In prayer, we gain knowledge of self and knowledge of God. Fruitful prayer cannot solely be vocal prayer, because the danger is that we will simply repeat words without understanding what we are saying or loving the One to whom we are speaking. Those who are wedded solely to vocal prayer say a certain number of Our Fathers and imagine that they have fulfilled their goal. The goal, however, is deeper communion with God, and this cannot be accomplished simply by saying words. But we should not abandon vocal prayer, because then we might not pray at all. The best thing is that "while she says the words she should make an effort to concentrate on my love, pondering at the same time her own sins and the blood of my only-begotten Son."[47] God instructs Catherine not to think of specific sins and not to focus on sins without at the same time recalling God's mercy. In prayer, God's love must have center stage. If we practice vocal prayer in this way, we will "advance from imperfect vocal prayer to perfect mental prayer."[48] This happens when we begin with vocal prayer and wait for God to make himself present to us, so that we enter into mental prayer. We know when our life of prayer is deepening when we find ourselves loving more and increasing in desire for God.

Indeed, holy desire for God is "continual prayer;" vocal and mental prayer concretizes what we should be desiring at all times. Since prayer is fundamentally love, every good word or deed is a prayer. Our whole lives should be a prayer. St. Paul teaches, "Rejoice always, pray constantly, give thanks in all circumstances; for this is

---

[44] Ibid., 231.
[45] See Catherine of Siena, *The Dialogue*, p. 125.
[46] Ibid., p. 122.
[47] Ibid., p. 124.
[48] Ibid., p. 125.

the will of God in Christ Jesus for you" (1 Thess. 5.16-18). With this passage in mind, Catherine emphasizes that "charity is continual prayer" but adds that we should not therefore abandon "actual prayer."[49] We need ordinary prayer if our lives are to manifest continual prayer. As a stimulus to holiness in the priesthood, for example, she calls upon priests to undertake "nightly vigils and the solemn and devout praying of the Office," along with "constant devoted prayer."[50] She invokes the example of the apostles and other saintly priests and bishops who offered God "the fragrant incense of eager longing and constant humble prayer."[51]

Writing to her brother, Jane de Chantal encourages him to pray in his own words, "speaking to our Lord sincerely, lovingly, confidently, and simply, as your heart dictates."[52] This kind of prayer will enable him to recognize himself as a child who can speak to his heavenly Father. Like a child, he should speak to God freely. The words that we speak in prayer should highlight our dependence on God for happiness and our assurance that God will see us through to union with him. We should repent our sins in simple words, and entrust ourselves entirely to God's mercy. The tone of prayer should be that of a relationship with a Father who is also our greatest friend.

Conclusion

Jesus reveals to us that we are God's beloved children. Through his Holy Spirit, God wishes to give us the inheritance of his Son. With such a generous and gracious Creator, we must surely be able to have a relationship with him. Yet people can live their entire lives wondering where God is and how to get in contact with him. People can easily despair of God's presence and even of God's existence. The result is that we cannot take communion with God for granted; we must instead work hard on learning how to pray. Teresa's advice that prayer is rooted in love, detachment, and humility provides us with the foundations for the life of prayer. She then helps us to

---

[49] Ibid., p. 127.
[50] Ibid., p. 236.
[51] Ibid., p. 229.
[52] Jane de Chantal, *Letters of Spiritual Direction*, p. 202.

understand how vocal prayer, such as the Lord's Prayer, can provide the entrance into the much deeper experience that is mental prayer. In mental prayer, our minds become caught up in a real conversation and communion with God. As we gain a sense of God through repentance and humility, we find ourselves increasingly able to recognize our friend and to experience his embrace of love, since he is perfect humility and can only be known by the humble. Even now, through the gift of contemplation, we are able to experience a foretaste of union with him. Let us press toward the goal of life!

10

Eternal life

Hildegard of Bingen has a mystical vision of the new heaven and new earth. She first describes the end of the world. The end of the world is not a mere destruction, but rather is a consummation that will occur when everything that God wills has been accomplished. Yet the end of the world also constitutes an experience of dying, a "death" of the entire universe. At the moment of the universe's death, all creation will undergo dissolution. Hildegard depicts this dissolution as involving chaos among the elements and the breaking up of ecosystems. She imagines that at the very end, "all creatures are set into violent motion, fire bursts out, the air dissolves, water runs off, the earth is shaken, lightnings burn, thunders crash, mountains are broken, forests fall, and whatever in air or water or earth is mortal gives up its life."[1] Just as in the process of dying our body and soul break apart and the integration of our bodily systems collapses, so also at the end of time the elements will rise up against each other. She envisions that "the fire displaces all the air, and the water engulfs all the earth."[2] The fire and water will end all life in the universe, but at the same time their purifying power will ensure that "whatever was foul in the world vanishes as if it had never been."[3] The universe will be renewed at the most basic level, that of the elements. A new freshness will be present due to the purification of the elements from which all the matter of the universe was composed.

After this purification, God will raise all humans from the dead. Their risen bodies will be composed of purified elements in which no trace of evil works or disorder remains. Hildegard signals here both

---

[1] Hildegard of Bingen, *Scivias*, p. 516.
[2] Ibid.
[3] Ibid.

continuity and discontinuity. Our risen bodies will be composed of earthly elements, but these elements will have undergone a profound purification. Something radically new will emerge, but without losing continuity with the old creation. Humans will rise "in soul and body, with no deformity or mutilation but intact in body and in gender."[4] All bodies will be beautiful, but beauty will be measured primarily in spiritual terms. Our risen bodies will be translucent to our souls, and the spiritual health of our souls will appear through our bodies. The bodies that have brightness will be those of the saints. While the saints will shine with spiritual beauty, the damned will have dull bodies that will lack inner illumination.

Thus our bodies will become spiritual; rather than being distinguished by external appearance, we will be distinguished by the spiritual condition of our souls. We will no longer be judged by externals, because our very bodiliness will reveal the beauty (or lack thereof) of our souls. The beauty of our souls comes from the works that we have done, and indeed these works will in some sense be visible in our risen bodies. In earthly life, sometimes the works we have done are visible in our faces, but this is not always the case. We can often conceal from others the bad deeds that we are doing. In eternal life, our bodies will make manifest what we have done; nothing will be concealed.

The character of our works flows from faith and charity. When all humans rise from the dead, Hildegard considers that three kinds of bodies will be visible. Some bodies will reveal that the person lacked faith. The lack of any faith means that the person freely chose, while on earth, to reject God. Other bodies will reveal that the person had faith, but these bodies will themselves be differentiated. Some persons of faith lacked charity and refused to do the works of faith. Their bodies will bear the sign of faith but will otherwise appear murky. They will lack the illumination they should have had, even though their possession of faith will not go unnoticed. These people have freely chosen to be damned. Other persons of faith possessed charity. Through their clean consciences, they will "shine with the radiance of wisdom."[5]

---

[4] Ibid., p. 517.
[5] Ibid.

At the resurrection, Jesus Christ will come to judge the entire human race. How will he make himself visible? Hildegard suggests that he will look different when viewed by the damned than when viewed by the saved. He will be bright with eternal glory, but a cloud will hide this glory from the damned. The point is that the brightness of Jesus' glory cannot be seen by the damned in the final judgment, no more than they were able to see it during their earthly lives. Their clouded spiritual sight is precisely the disorder that has ruined them. Jesus is qualified to judge because as the Son of God he is Creator of all things, and as man he judges all creation from the inside. If only the Creator were the judge, then the judgment would be extrinsic; if only a man were the judge, then the judge would not have authority to put all deeds in their proper place. Since the judge is both God and man, he is fully qualified for his office. He brings all things, whether visible or invisible, into judgment. Prior to the final judgment, human affairs often seem badly ordered: why does this just man suffer terribly, while his oppressor seems to thrive? Hildegard makes clear, then, that to judge the world is to put things to rights, to "put them in their proper order."[6] At the final judgment, Jesus establishes the true order of all things, the order that God wills from the beginning and that is not apparent until Jesus brings it about.

When Jesus places before himself all those who had faith, the works of faith become evident. These works, often hidden during the course of human history, now appear as the true heart of history. Having performed works of faith through love, the just are the "flowers" that Jesus gathers from human history. These flowers of Christ "shine out in radiance."[7] They are the saints from every age, before and after Christ's earthly life. Hildegard mentions first the patriarchs, prophets, and apostles, and then she mentions those who imitated Christ through martyrdom, preaching, and virginity. Their lives involved great mortifications, which made their souls beautiful like radiant flowers by stimulating their humility and charity. They made themselves small and weak for Christ's sake, and now they are recognized as the great ones of human history. They imitated Christ not because they wanted to be great in the world's

---

[6] Ibid., p. 518.
[7] Ibid.

eyes, but at the final judgment their greatness—their humility—will be present for all to see.

Hildegard envisions a celestial silence out of which Christ speaks his judgment. The solemnity of the moment interrupts the music of the divine praise. History is so important that all, even the angels, wish to hear Christ's judgment. Indeed, one can see that Christ's judgment is itself a divine praise, because he praises God for the just in giving them eternal life. He condemns the wicked who freely and permanently chose themselves over God. Since not all of the actions of the just were good, Christ's judgment is not merely a setting to rights of the wicked by means of condemnation. Christ's judgment must also bring to justice the evil deeds of the just. In Hildegard's view, the judgment of the wicked who had faith will be different from the judgment of those who rejected faith. Christ's judgment reflects the degrees to which persons were united to his body, the Church. Unbelievers receive a judgment proper to those who lacked connection with Christ. By rejecting faith (and baptism after its institution), they chose to remain in their sins, preeminently the sin of false worship. Although some of those who had faith will be condemned due to their lack of charity, nonetheless their bond with Christ will be acknowledged at the judgment.

At the completion of the final judgment, according to Hildegard, all change in the universe's elements will come to an end. There will no longer be winds or storms, because the universe will now reflect the stability and spiritual beauty of the saints. The elements of the new heaven and new earth will project glorious stability: air will be pure and clear, fire will be bright but not burning hot or destructive, water will be calm and no longer a threat to drown people; earth will be flat, firm, and not quake-prone. The stars will not roam the sky; they will add to the glory and beauty of the new creation, but they will not revolve because day and night are no more (cf. Rev 22.5). All that remains is "day" because God will bathe everything in his glorious light. Nothing transitory will remain; all that remains will share in some way in eternal life. Put succinctly, "the world will have ended." [8] God will bring about the fullness of true peace. Hildegard observes that "the elect will become splendid with the splendor of

---

[8] Ibid., p. 520.

eternity."[9] The peace of eternal life is marked by light and by music, the harmonious and glorious sound of joy and praise.

Regarding hell, Hildegard speaks of it as an eternal death, in which the damned are swallowed up. Yet hell does not annihilate the fallen angels and proud people. The groaning of the damned contrasts with the joyful praise of the redeemed. This groaning goes beyond the pain and frustration that we can understand on earth. Hildegard sums up her doctrine of eternal life by quoting Jesus' words in Matthew 25.46: "And these shall go into everlasting punishment; but the just into life everlasting."[10]

Does Hildegard think that the above portrait, which she depicts in human concepts, conveys in a literal manner the aspects of the new heaven and new earth? Although she thinks that these things will happen and that she has truthfully expressed them, she warns against reading her words in a literalistic manner. At the end of her mystical vision, God commands: "But let the one who has ears sharp to hear inner meanings ardently love My reflection and pant after My words, and inscribe them in his soul and conscience."[11] The "inner meanings" here have to do with the victory of love; we are to ardently love this victory and to desire it for ourselves in all our actions.

Hildegard includes one final mystical vision, that of the citizens of heaven and their songs of praise and prayer. The first song praises Mary as mother of "the glorious Flower."[12] After this, she hears a song in praise of the orders of the angels "who behold the heart of the Father,/And see the Ancient of Days spring forth in the fountain,/And His inner power appear like a face from His heart."[13] The next songs praise the patriarchs, prophets, apostles, martyrs, confessors, and virgins. In praising these people, as in praising Mary and the angels, the songs focus on the way in which they reflect and participate in God. For example, the song that praises the virgins proclaims that their "clear serenity shines in the Wheel of Godhead."[14] In eternal life, we will rejoice in what God has done

---

[9] Ibid., p. 519.
[10] Ibid., p. 520.
[11] Ibid., p. 521.
[12] Ibid., p. 525.
[13] Ibid.
[14] Ibid., p. 528.

in and through his creatures. We will celebrate the beauty and glory of the creation that God has brought to fulfillment.

Since at present the final judgment has not yet happened, the songs of the angels and saints also contain prayers for those who are alive on earth. These songs sorrow over the Fall and over the sinfulness of humans; they praise God's glorious compassion and God's victory over the devil through Jesus Christ. They intercede for humans by urging the victory of the virtues in souls. One song takes the form of a dialogue between the soul and the virtues; in the very midst of the song, the devil tempts the soul, but the virtues overcome the devil and give praise to Christ and the Father. Here we see a connection between the angels and saints in heaven and humans who are presently living on earth. The angels and saints are continuously praying for the victory of the virtues in our lives, and when we are victorious they rejoice. Because human life is a spiritual battle, Hildegard states that "[p]raises must be offered unceasingly to the Supernal Creator with heart and mouth, for by His grace he sets on heavenly thrones not only those who stand erect but those who bend and fall."[15] Many people who are presently turning away from God, to the sadness of the angels and saints, are indeed among the elect; they "will be led to blessed joy by the divine power, and know the mysteries no human mind can know that bows down to the earth."[16]

The angels and saints know who are the elect, because they see God and know his glorious plan. Life after death, then, is no mere continuation of history. The fullness of God's plan is revealed to the saints. Thus their song already has perfect harmony, because they understand the whole and love God's work of salvation. The song is ultimately about the glory and joy of sharing in God's life. They sing in praise of "what the Word has shown."[17] Their song reflects the perfect deification of body and soul, and the unity of God and humans that is accomplished through Jesus Christ. The words of the song express bodiliness/humanity, and the harmonious music expresses soul/divinity.

---

[15] Ibid., p. 532.
[16] Ibid.
[17] Ibid., p. 533.

Hildegard concludes that believers on earth need to join in this heavenly music by singing songs of praise, as well as songs of lamentation. We should obey the command of the psalm, "Praise Him with the sound of trumpets; praise Him with psaltery and harp. Praise Him with timbrel and dance; praise Him with stringed instruments and flute. Praise Him on high-sounding cymbals; praise Him on cymbals of joy; let every spirit praise the Lord" (Ps. 150.3.5). Indeed the Church is already singing this heavenly music; the Church on earth already participates in the song of the blessed who live with God. This song provides the pattern of the life of virtue, and this song rejoices in the conversion of sinners and in the perseverance of the saints. By singing holy songs, our hearts are softened, and we weep for our sins and strengthen our desire for life eternal. The heavenly song indicates the working of the grace of the Holy Spirit. Hildegard considers that the various musical instruments noted by the psalmist symbolize the different ways we can praise God: through our minds, through devotion, through mortification, through martyrdom, through preaching, through virginity, through conversion, through the virtues. Above all, the path to God is charity and humility, because God himself is humble love.

What happens, however, if we die before we have become perfected in charity? When we reflect on our spiritual lives, we often recognize how much more purified we need to be in order to love God and neighbor as fully as we should. After we die, assuming we truly possess charity, does God continue to perfect our hearts?

Catherine of Genoa experienced God perfecting her prior to her death. She felt "the fiery love of God, a love that consumed her, cleansing and purifying all, so that once quitted this life she could appear forthwith in God's presence."[18] This experience awakened her to the situation of souls who die with charity but without having been fully cleansed. God cannot simply leave souls as they are at the time of death. Even if they die with charity, they need to be perfected in order to take the place in the body of Christ that God has prepared for them by giving them faith, hope, and charity. Although we are all called to be perfect, it is quite evident

---

[18] Catherine of Genoa, *Purgation and Purgatory, The Spiritual Dialogue*, trans. Serge Hughes (New York: Paulist Press, 1979), p. 71.

experientially that few of us strive wholeheartedly toward the perfection of love. When we die, we may love God and neighbor but we are quite far from being great models of self-giving love, great saints. If death itself were sufficient as a purgation, then there would be no real incentive to strive to be perfect in our earthly lives. The problem, in short, has to do with charitable people who are only moderately charitable at the time of their death. Having already chosen God with love, such people need to become fully charitable but do not need a second temporal life. Their choice has been made but needs to be completed. If God's purpose is to perfect us so that we are fully holy, how can God do this?

In Catherine of Genoa's experience of purgation here on earth, she realized that what perfects us is the fire of God's love. What causes our purgation after death is our encounter with God's fiery love. Since this is so, those who are experiencing purgatory after death do not rebel against it. Rather, since they already love God, they rejoice to be coming gradually to a deeper union with God's love. Indeed, Catherine writes that "[s]uch is their joy in God's will, in His pleasure, that they have no concern for themselves but dwell only on their joy in God's ordinance, in having Him do what He will."[19] Since God's will is pure goodness, they experience as good the action of his will upon them.

But don't people in purgatory suffer? It would seem that purgation involves painful suffering. Catherine denies, however, that people undergoing purgatory experience a form of suffering that makes them regret being in purgatory. She argues instead that their wills are sufficiently conformed to God's so that they are happy to be where God wills them to be. They do not dwell on regrets about their earthly life or wish that they were already in heaven. To wish to be where God does not will us to be is a sin, however minor such a sin might be. The souls in purgatory, having died in charity, no longer sin. They are not living a second life in which they choose anew between sinning and doing the right thing. On the contrary, God has united their wills with his. What causes their purgation is not further small sins on their part, but rather their encounter in love with the glorious fire of divine love. This encounter purifies them painfully by stretching their ability to love, but they rejoice in this

---

[19] Ibid.

holy pain. To use another metaphor, God strips them of everything, no matter how slight, that prevents them from full openness to his fiery love.

What then of the passage of death? Catherine connects it with purgation to the extent that she thinks that in death's painful passage, we are aware of the sins for which we will be undergoing purgation, an awareness that leaves us as soon as we arrive at the divine fire. Death unites us to God's indescribably powerful love, but we are generally not yet ready for this love. Our intellect and will, in purgatory, are filled simply with the joy of loving God and of desiring to love him more. Purgatory is an experience of ever-increasing joy, as God dissolves everything that limits our love. As Catherine puts it, "The more rust of sin is consumed by fire, the more the soul responds to that love, and its joy increases."[20]

But if purgatory is so joyful, do the souls experiencing purgation experience no suffering? Catherine thinks that they do in fact suffer, although as they are more purified, they suffer less. They are able to suffer joyfully, however, for two reasons. First, the souls in purgatory are united to God's will, and so they rejoice in God's will being done in them. Second, their suffering arises primarily from the fact that they are interiorly prevented from loving God perfectly. Catherine repeatedly emphasizes that the souls in purgatory are not sinning. Their wills are united to God; if their wills were evil, then they would be in hell. Even so, their wills do not love as much as they should. They do not love as much as they need to love in order to partake fully in beatitude. Since their wills are already good, they are able to experience God's presence in a way that gradually makes their wills perfectly good.

What is the difference between a good will and a perfectly good will, if not sin? Because the souls in purgatory have rejected sin, they cannot sin. Yet their wills retain what Catherine calls "the rust and deformity of sin."[21] The image of rust helps us to conceive a will that is good, but not as perfectly good as it should be. A sword that has rusted may still be sharp if we clean off the rust. A rusted sword is not necessarily a dull sword, once the rust has been cleaned away. Similarly, a "rusted" will need not be sinful. In this case, rust means

---

[20] Ibid., p. 72.
[21] Ibid., p. 76.

a lack of full desire for beatitude. The will loves, but it does not love as it should. Such a will cannot yet sustain the glorious vision of God.

Catherine also gives the image of a hungry person seeking bread who comes close to this bread without yet being able to eat it. The pangs of hunger grow worse the closer the person gets to the delicious-smelling bread, even as the person also becomes increasingly joyful. The suffering of the souls in purgatory is like "the waiting for the bread that will take away their hunger."[22] Before the soul can consume the bread of heaven—the vision of God—it must be stretched so that it desires this bread as fully as it must in order to receive it. Catherine observes that "the soul that has but the slightest imperfection would rather throw itself into a thousand hells than appear thus before the divine presence."[23]

Having made clear that the souls in purgatory are focused on loving God and are not suffering for ongoing sin, Catherine grants that these souls know that "something in them displeases God" and that something "blocks them on their way to God."[24] God knows and sees the soul as it should be, in its purity of love. In purgatory, then, God's love brings about this purity, so that "the soul feels itself melting in the fire of that love of its sweet God, for He will not cease until He has brought the soul to its perfection."[25] God's love burns away all that impedes the soul from rising fully to God in response to his love. The souls in purgatory still possess some residual resistance to God's love, and it is this resistance that is melted away so that they can give themselves fully. Their awareness of this resistance causes the suffering of the souls in purgatory. In this way, we can see how "in purgatory great joy and great suffering do not exclude one another."[26]

Catherine also employs the image of gold that is purified by fire until it contains no dross and is absolutely pure (24-carat). Her emphasis, again, is that it is not the fire of divine love that causes suffering: God's love causes rejoicing in the souls in purgatory. Their suffering comes from the fact that because of their imperfection,

---

[22] Ibid., p. 77.
[23] Ibid., p. 78.
[24] Ibid.
[25] Ibid., p. 79.
[26] Ibid., p. 82.

they cannot yet fully experience the love that they desire. By the operation of his love, God removes even our most hidden flaws. Catherine remarks that "[t]hings man considers perfect leave much to be desired in the eyes of God."[27] Only God can fully transform us so that seeing him will not blind us by his brightness. The souls in purgatory recognize this and they focus entirely on God's love, in complete dependence on God for their restoration to perfect justice. In this regard Catherine warns against underestimating, in this life, the difficulty of being perfectly cleansed of sins. She underscores that "[i]f God's mercy did not temper His justice—that justice which has been satisfied with the blood of Jesus Christ—one sin alone would deserve a thousand eternal hells."[28]

Catherine praises God for enabling the soul, by grace, "to participate in His life, to become one with Him, in the sharing of His goodness."[29] This is our goal, and we can experience it already now, even if not fully. She makes clear that God does not bar the door to heaven for anyone; heaven is wide open, and the only impediments come from our side. The "[a]ll-merciful God stands there with His arms open, waiting to receive us into His glory."[30] Nor does God construct hell, except in the sense that God mitigates it once we have chosen it. Hell, says Catherine, "is evil will," that is to say the perversion that consists in opposing the love of God.[31] Since there is no second temporal life, the choice we make for or against God in this life is permanent. Life after death is not a continuation of this life with its choices. Instead, the life to come is radically different because we encounter there the fullness of our choices. Although the damned suffer forever in hell, however, God mitigates the intensity of their suffering. Indeed, the very existence of hell already limits the intensity of their suffering, because punishment is the work of God's justice. Nothing is more horrible than the absence of justice. As Catherine states, "Were the sinful soul not there where the justice of God wills it, the soul would be in a still greater hell. Then it would be out of that divine order which is a

---

[27] Ibid., p. 81.
[28] Ibid., p. 84.
[29] Ibid., p. 86.
[30] Ibid., p. 78.
[31] Ibid., p. 74.

part of God's mercy."[32] God does not intervene to send souls to hell. Rather, having turned away from God, the soul itself at the moment of death goes to hell by its own volition, just as souls that love God choose to be united with him in heaven.

Mechthild of Magdeburg reports of a mystical vision in which she sees St. Hildegund, who had died some decades earlier, receive her glory. What happens when God fully unites a person to himself? Mechthild sees Hildegund adorned as a bride before the Father's throne. Mechthild describes this adornment through symbolic numbers joined to regal imagery. In the vision, Hildegund has "three mantles draped over her and wore on her head seven crowns, and the nine choirs offered her special praise."[33] The three mantles symbolize her martyrdom, her good works, and her supreme love. The seven crowns symbolize her constancy, faith, fidelity, mercy, understanding, love, and virginity. Each of them has a garland symbolizing chastity. The nine choirs praise her virtues, and the angelic Seraphim and Thrones also praise her love and beauty. To enter into heavenly glory, then, is to receive glorious praise. This praise is not for what the world values, but instead is for what God values and has enabled us to do. We receive praise for having imitated Christ. To enter into heaven is to be fully a creature, and at the same time to be exalted by the grace of the Holy Spirit. We become the creatures that we were meant to be, and this restoration is a work of grace in us that makes us God's bride.

Mechthild also has a vision of heaven itself. She first sees the Lord Jesus and rejoices in his wisdom and scars. He looks her in the face and kisses her, and she sees the wonders of eternal life, "God's house."[34] She imagines it in terms of a church with choir benches. Where Satan once sat will be filled by John the Baptist. Above the choirs is the vaulted throne of God, where the Father, incarnate Son, and Holy Spirit sit. Mary is uniquely united to her Son on the throne, and the apostles sit nearby. The highest choirs are filled with virgins, martyrs, preachers, and continent married persons. Each of the blessed will have a distinct personal relationship of praise with the Father, the Son, and the Holy Spirit. Marching forth

---

[32] Ibid., p. 77.

[33] Mechthild of Magdeburg, *The Flowing Light of the Godhead*, p. 84.

[34] Ibid., p. 102.

from their choir benches, the blessed dance in a circle around the throne of God, and they "sing the truth effortlessly with joy, as God had entrusted it to them."[35] Each group—preachers, martyrs, and so forth—sings a different song in accord with the special graces they received on earth. The dignity of the blessed is not their own, but instead "[t]hey rest in God's strength and flow in bliss, keeping themselves in God's breath, as does the air in the sun."[36] They are preparing for the heavenly banquet of the bride with the Bridegroom, when they will be fully glorified. Mechthild adds a particularly important detail: "Towering above everything that was ever in heaven is a sense of wonder," the wonder and delight that the blessed experience in seeing God and in "the special intimacy that unceasingly exists between God and each individual soul."[37]

She knows that this vision is not meant to be taken literally. Rather she asks us to find in her description of the vision, the meaning that God intends for it to have. Eternal life is connected to our earthly lives; our glory there accords with the kind of love that we have shown here. We are to become the temple of God and the bride of God. To gain eternal life requires learning to rest entirely in God's strength. We must gaze on him with wonder, and receive God's gaze and kiss. We enjoy now, and will enjoy infinitely more profoundly then, a personal relationship with the three divine Persons, Father, Son, and Holy Spirit. Our entrance into eternal life comes through our encounter with Jesus Christ and our love of his scars, since his humble love and self-sacrificial Pasch are our path of restoration and exaltation.

Conclusion

As Mechthild says, "Towering above everything that was ever in heaven is a sense of wonder." We are purely God's gift. He wondrously loved us into existence and loved us even unto death on the Cross, supreme humiliation. He is lofty and infinite, and yet he is a mad lover who gives himself entirely. To know him, we must learn to be

---

[35] Ibid., p. 104.
[36] Ibid., p. 105.
[37] Ibid., p. 106.

like him, and he comes himself into our lives to show us (in Christ and by the Spirit) how to do this. The wondrous mystery that he is in no way a creature, that he is infinite, unbounded triune fullness of all interpersonal perfection, now is united to the wondrous mystery that he has made things to participate in his goodness. Come, let us rejoice at his table!

Conclusion

Flannery O'Connor observed about some of her visitors that "they do all the talking and they have fantastic but very positive ideas about how everything is and ought to be; and they are mighty sophisticated on the outside. The visits leave me exhausted and yearning to go sit with the chickens."[1] By contrast, the women mystical theologians are sophisticated on the inside. They introduce us to the triune God of love whose gifting is wondrous beyond expression. Their knowledge of Jesus is possible not for the plastic saint but for the real saint.

Imagine if we could sit at a table with the women mystical theologians. What would they say to us? I imagine that they would be both sterner and more loving than we could expect. They would recognize our sins as they recognized theirs; and they would show us that when God looks at us, he looks at us with love. Indeed, God has created and redeemed us with such generosity that we hardly know what to make of it. In creation, in Israel, in Jesus Christ, and in the Eucharist, he hands himself over to us with the purpose of leading us to share in his infinite wisdom and love. The Church is the communion of love, a communion of gift—but not in a sentimental sense. In our fallen condition, we do not love easily. O'Connor speaks both of the cost of grace, which requires self-sacrificial love, and of "the patience of Christ in history and not with select people but with very ordinary ones—as ordinary as the vacillating children of Israel and the fishermen apostles."[2] So that we might learn love, God ensures that we receive his truth and sacramental grace from the hands of other sinners, as a community rather than solely as individuals. Relating to Jesus cannot be separated from relating to his friends, because that is the kind of lover he is. God

---

[1] Flannery O'Connor, *The Habit of Being: Letters of Flannery O'Connor*, ed. Sally Fitzgerald (New York: Farrar, Straus & Giroux, 1979), p. 249.
[2] Ibid., p. 337.

is himself triune wisdom and love: he is the unity-in-communion that we glimpse in our deepest moments of personal intimacy. God is uncreated; he can name himself simply by saying "I am," with all the power and wisdom and love stored up in that name. But God's greatness is infinite humility and infinite love.

The humorist Erma Bombeck reminds us that "Life has a way of accelerating as we get older. The days get shorter, and the list of promises to ourselves gets longer. One morning, we awaken, and all we have to show for our lives is a litany of 'I'm going to,' 'I plan on' and 'Someday, when things are settled down a bit.'"[3] She goes on to jokingly apply this to dieting: "I got to thinking one day about all those women on the *Titanic* who passed up dessert at dinner that fateful night in an effort to cut back. From then on, I've tried to be a bit more flexible."[4] Of course her joke contains a serious point. Temporal life and love do not last very long. Here and now, however, we can receive a relationship with the divine All Good, the Mad Lover. We can focus our promises and plans upon this Lover. The women mystical theologians did just this, and they were not disappointed. The love of God is infinitely good.

Let me conclude with a conversion story. Reading the psalms while in prison for political protesting, but before becoming a Catholic, Dorothy Day found herself inclining toward God. This experience was not something she immediately welcomed. Rather, as she says, "all the while I read, my pride was fighting on. I did not want to go to God in defeat and sorrow. I did not want to depend on Him. I was like the child that wants to walk by itself, I kept brushing away the hand that held me up. I tried to persuade myself that I was reading for literary enjoyment."[5] Later when she began praying more regularly, she was surprised to find that she was praying from happiness and gratitude rather than from fear or the desire to gain something. At the time, she was in a common-law marriage, and she was pregnant. She began to plan to become a Catholic and to have her infant daughter baptized; to do so she had to give up living in her common-law relationship, because the man refused marriage.

---

[3] Erma Bombeck, *Forever, Erma: Best-Loved Writing from America's Favorite Humorist* (Kansas City, MO: Andrews McMeel Publishing, 1996), p. 244.

[4] Ibid.

[5] Dorothy Day, *The Long Loneliness: The Autobiography of Dorothy Day* (New York: Harper & Row, 1981), p. 81.

She notes that when she first received the sacraments, she felt no interior consolation; rather, she simply "wanted to be poor, chaste and obedient. I wanted to die in order to live, to put off the old man and put on Christ. I loved, in other words, and like all women in love, I wanted to be united to my love."[6] Like all women—and like all men. She found herself choosing to give everything up in order to be united to Jesus Christ in his body, the Church.

To study Catholic theology is to gain knowledge about the realities that set her heart aflame. Let us begin!

---

[6] Ibid., p. 149.

INDEX